m dern $LAVERY

AND THE GLOBAL ECONOMY

IDEAS in C NFLICT

Gary E. McCuen

GARY McCUEN publications inc.

411 Mallalieu Drive
Hudson, Wisconsin 54016
Phone (715) 386-7113

Illustration and Photo Credits

Carol★Simpson 25, 57, 121, 159; Jeff MacNelly 139; UNICEF 33, 47, 73, 79, 87, 91, 97, 105, 109, 113; U.S. Department of Agriculture 64; Richard Wright 152, 167.

© 1998 by Gary E. McCuen Publications, Inc.
411 Mallalieu Drive, Hudson, Wisconsin 54016

(715) 386-7113

International Standard Book Number
0-86596-145X
Printed in the United States of America

CONTENTS

Ideas in Conflict

Chapter 1 MARGINAL WORKERS AND GLOBAL SLAVERY: AN OVERVIEW

1. PRISONERS AND PROFITS: CHINA'S
SLAVE LABOR SYSTEM
Harry Wu   9

2. BURMA: SLAVE NATION
John Pilger   15

3. MADE IN THE USA: SWEATSHOPS
EXPLOIT IMMIGRANT WOMEN
William Branigin   21

4. THE LABOR OF CHILDREN
UNICEF   29

5. WOMEN SLAVES OF THE SEX TRADE
Alice Leuchtag   36

6. THE INVISIBLE SOLDIERS: CHILD COMBATANTS
The Center for Defense Information   43

WHAT IS EDITORIAL BIAS?
Reasoning Skill Activity   51

Chapter 2 SLAVE LABOR, CHILD LABOR, AND THE MAQUILADORES

7. THE SLAVES WE RENT
A.V. Krebs   54

8. AMERICANS WON'T DO THE WORK
James S. Holt   62

9. STOLEN YOUTH – DEGRADED CHILDREN
Robert Weissman   69

10. BLANKET CONDEMNATION HELPS NO ONE   77
        Chris Brazier

11. SWEATSHOPS FOR THE WORLD'S POOR   84
        Joyce Bowers

12. OPPORTUNITY SHOPS FOR THE DISPOSSESSED   89
        Hans F. Sennholz

13. RETAILERS' RACE TO THE BOTTOM   94
        Charles Kernaghan

14. RETAILERS' OPPOSITION TO EXPLOITATION   101
        Robert Hall and Kathie Lee Gifford

15. END CHILD LABOR: BAN THEIR PRODUCTS   107
        Christopher H. Smith

16. END CHILD LABOR: BUY THEIR PRODUCTS   111
        William Anderson

     INTERPRETING EDITORIAL CARTOONS   116
        Reasoning Skill Activity

Chapter 3 **THE GLOBAL ECONOMY: ECONOMIC GROWTH AND HUMAN RIGHTS**

17. INTERNATIONAL LABOR STANDARDS: 118
     THE POINT
        Neil Kearney

18. INTERNATIONAL LABOR STANDARDS: 125
     THE COUNTERPOINT
        Jagdish Bhagwati

19. MOST FAVORED NATION TRADE STATUS   131
     WILL PROMOTE PROGRESS IN CHINA
        Madeleine K. Albright

20. MOST FAVORED NATION STATUS   136
     MUST BE DENIED
        Representative Richard A. Gephardt

21. THE NORTH AMERICAN FREE TRADE AGREEMENT: 142
    A SUCCESS
    The Clinton Administration

22. THE NORTH AMERICAN FREE TRADE AGREEMENT: 148
    A FAILED EXPERIMENT
    Economic Policy Institute, et al.

23. ENDLESS GROWTH IS OBSOLETE   156
    David C. Korten

24. GLOBALIZATION LEADS TO PROGRESS   164
    Thomas d'Aquino

BIBLIOGRAPHY: Useful Research Materials   173

INDEX   175

REASONING SKILL DEVELOPMENT

These activities may be used as individualized study guides for students in libraries and resource centers or as discussion catalysts in small group and classroom discussions.

1. What is EDITORIAL BIAS?   51

2. Interpreting EDITORIAL CARTOONS   116

IDEAS
in CONFLICT

This series features ideas in conflict on political, social, and moral issues. It presents counterpoints, debates, opinions, commentary, and analysis for use in libraries and classrooms. Each title in the series uses one or more of the following basic elements:

Introductions that present an issue overview giving historic background and/or a description of the controversy.

Counterpoints and debates carefully chosen from publications, books, and position papers on the political right and left to help librarians and teachers respond to requests that treatment of public issues be fair and balanced.

Symposiums and forums that go beyond debates that can polarize and oversimplify. These present commentary from across the political spectrum that reflect how complex issues attract many shades of opinion.

A global emphasis with foreign perspectives and surveys on various moral questions and political issues that will help readers to place subject matter in a less culture-bound and ethnocentric frame of reference. In an ever-shrinking and interdependent world, understanding and cooperation are essential. Many issues are global in nature and can be effectively dealt with only by common efforts and international understanding.

Reasoning skill study guides and discussion activities provide ready-made tools for helping with critical reading and evaluation of content. The guides and activities deal with one or more of the following:

RECOGNIZING AUTHOR'S POINT OF VIEW

INTERPRETING EDITORIAL CARTOONS

VALUES IN CONFLICT

WHAT IS EDITORIAL BIAS?

WHAT IS SEX BIAS?

WHAT IS POLITICAL BIAS?

WHAT IS ETHNOCENTRIC BIAS?

WHAT IS RACE BIAS?

WHAT IS RELIGIOUS BIAS?

*From across **the political spectrum** varied sources are presented for research projects and classroom discussions. Diverse opinions in the series come from magazines, newspapers, syndicated columnists, books, political speeches, foreign nations, and position papers by corporations and nonprofit institutions.*

About the Editor

Gary E. McCuen is an editor and publisher of anthologies for libraries and discussion materials for schools and colleges. His publications have specialized in social, moral and political conflict. They include books, pamphlets, cassettes, tabloids, filmstrips and simulation games, most of them created from his many years of experience in teaching and educational publishing.

CHAPTER 1

MARGINAL WORKERS AND GLOBAL SLAVERY: AN OVERVIEW

1. PRISONERS AND PROFITS: CHINA'S   9
   SLAVE LABOR SYSTEM
   Harry Wu

2. BURMA: SLAVE NATION   15
   John Pilger

3. MADE IN THE USA: SWEATSHOPS   21
   EXPLOIT IMMIGRANT WOMEN
   William Branigin

4. THE LABOR OF CHILDREN   29
   UNICEF

5. WOMEN SLAVES OF THE SEX TRADE   36
   Alice Leuchtag

6. THE INVISIBLE SOLDIERS: CHILD COMBATANTS   43
   The Center for Defense Information

   WHAT IS EDITORIAL BIAS?   51
   Reasoning Skill Activity

PRISONERS AND PROFITS: CHINA'S SLAVE LABOR SYSTEM

Harry Wu

Harry Wu spent 19 years as a political prisoner in the Chinese forced labor system. He now lives in the United States and has researched and publicized the forced labor system for the Laogai Research Foundation in Milpitas, California.

■ POINTS TO CONSIDER

1. Discuss Mr. Wu's experience in the Laogai.

2. Has the work or purpose of the forced labor changed over the years? Explain.

3. According to Wu's description, summarize the organization of the forced labor system in China.

4. What has been the scope of the system since 1949?

Excerpted from the testimony of Harry Wu before the Subcommittee on International Operations and Human Rights of the House of Representatives Committee on International Relations, April 3, 1995.

The Chinese government not only has engaged in the political persecution of its citizens, but it has also forced these prisoners to labor for the profit of the Communist regime.

I was born in Shanghai in 1937. During my second year of college, in 1957, the students were encouraged by the Communist Party to express their opinions and concerns about the direction of the country. Although I initially kept quiet, in the end I offered a few criticisms, including my opinion that the Soviet invasion of Hungary in 1956 was a violation of international law and my feeling that the Communists were treating the common people as second-class citizens. Following my comments, I was arrested and sentenced in 1958, without a trial, to life in a Reeducation Through Labor camp because of my "poor political attitude."

In 1961, after I had served three years already, the government reduced my life sentence to three years. After I served my new three-year term, yet imprisoned since 1958, the authorities decided to extend my sentence again because of my reform performance. In 1964, I was given an indefinite extension. I was held in the forced labor camps without a trial until December 1969. At that time, however, I was not released from the forced labor camp and allowed to return home. Instead, I was forced to resettle permanently at a Laogai coal mine and serve as a forced-job-placement personnel. I was finally released from the Laogai system in 1979.

I spent my 19 years in the Laogai at twelve different Laogai camps. I was forced to do slave labor at an agricultural farm, a chemical factory, a steel plant, and a coal mine. I was regularly denied food and nearly starved to death. Torture permanently damaged my back. I had my arm broken during a beating. I had to become a beast in the Laogai so that I could fight to survive day after day. Today, all over the so-called new China, there are millions still fighting to survive in the Laogai.

The term *laogaidui* is a blanket phrase to describe the entire Chinese labor reform camp system. The system comprises a national complex of prisons which in terms of scope, numbers of camps and prisoners, degree of cruelty, and violation of human rights far surpasses the terrible Soviet Gulag.

LAOGAI

Laogai is literally translated into English as "reform through labor." This phrase is not only accurate to describe the role of the labor reform system, but also exactly describes the daily lives of the prisoners in the camps. The Laogai was deliberately erected by the Chinese Communist government "to punish and reform all counter-revolutionaries and other criminals" whereby "the process of labor reform of criminals...is essentially an effective method of purging and eliminating all criminals and counter-revolutionaries." Those are exact quotes from Chinese Public Security Bureau authorities in the 1950s.

Initially in the 1950s, the entrepreneurial management of the Laogai was not very developed. One reason for this was the special emphasis placed at that time in maintaining social stability and support for the new regime by suppressing opposition. Another reason was that for the most part all Laogai work was directed towards railroad construction, mining, reclamation of wasteland, water conservation projects, and similar large-scale labor intensive projects that required no special management. The use of the Laogai prisoners in this type of work continues in the development projects of the Chinese inland provinces like Guangxi, Qinghai, Xinjiang, and Tibet. Many of China's mine enterprises are in fact Laogai camps. Water conservancy projects, like the ongoing Three Gorges Dam construction project, regularly use Laogai labor and construction materials like cement made at Laogai factories. The Loagai has contributed, and continues to contribute, thousands upon thousands of slave-like, manual laborers to the Communist government's development and modernization plans. But like the Chinese economy itself under Deng's leadership, the Laogai has been forced to diversify.

PRISONERS AND PROFITS

The Laogai system forces its prisoners to plant, harvest, engineer, manufacture and process any imaginable product that can be sold either domestically in the new Chinese consumer-based economy or in the international market. Laogai policies clearly state, "Our Laogai facilities are both special schools for reforming Laogai prisoners and special state-owned enterprises." These "special" Laogai enterprises have become an indispensable component of the national economy. Some Laogai enterprises, camouflaged under phony business names and advertised as "state-run enterprises," are well known both domestically and international-ly. The wealth the products from these Laogai enterprises add to the government's coffers is greater than that earned by many of the much written about and heavily subsidized state enterprises. They turn out about one-half of the nation's rubber products, one-third of the nation's tea, grapes for Remy Martin, coal for sale to Great Britain, press machines and diesel engines for sale to the United States, and many, many other goods. The Laogai is so productive, the Beijing government never encounters financial problems funding it. Under the government's "responsibility system," which forces all enterprises to become less dependent on the central government for capital support, the Laogai has been more productive than ever. And more profitable.

There can be no denial that this is clearly state-run slavery. The Chinese government not only has engaged in the political persecution of its citizens in condemning them to the Laogai, but it has also forced these prisoners to labor for the development and profit of the Communist regime.

When the Laogai has faltered in the face of new threats, the Communist government has simply broadened its application. The *laojiao* and *jiuye* policies are both components of the Laogai system that were created to satisfy immediate needs of the dictatorship.

LAOJIAO

Administratively a component of the Laogai, *laojiao* is translated "reeducation through labor," but that is only a cosmetic difference. The true significance of laojiao is that it is defined as the "highest administrative discipline." This means one can be sentenced to laojiao without any judicial hearing or trial whatsoever. Since laojiao prisoners are subject to both thought reform and reform through labor identical to that found in the Laogai camps for convicted prisoners, one can be arrested and sentenced for up to three years without the "inconvenience" of a trial.

The Communists publicly hide the laojiao by stating it is a part of the public social security and welfare system, but it remains administratively under the Public Security Ministry. According to official explanations, laojiao is not a criminal proceeding since it is "highest level administrative discipline." Laojiao subjects are not criminals; they are referred to as "personnel" or "students." Many laojiao facilities are referred to as "special schools." This duplicity on the part of the Communist regime has led to foreign misunderstanding of the true role of laojiao as an active component of the Laogai. Laojiao subjects are organized in exactly the same military fashion as convicted Laogai prisoners. Styles and methods of labor production and thought reform are exactly alike. Since laojiao prisoners are not called prisoners, they are paid very low wages to maintain this appearance. Their housing is supervised by Laogai administration and is essentially the same as the convicted Laogai prisoners. Food is controlled and rationed. Mail and visits from relatives are limited and strictly supervised. All packages are first opened and inspected and any items considered inappropriate are confiscated.

JIUYE

There is a popular saying in the Laogai that goes, "There is an end to Laogai or laojiao, but jiuye is forever." For many prisoners in the Laogai, in fact more than 90% of Laogai prisoners before 1980, there is never full release from the system. There is only forced-job-placement. The purpose of the forced-job-placement, or *jiuye*, policy is stated, "...to fully implement labor reform policies and ensure public security." Since nearly all Chinese rely on the government for job assignment or placement, a released prisoner must go where his job placement takes him. For many, they simply remain at the Laogai camp and continue working as a jiuye person. It is thus rather apparent that jiuye is part of, or an extension of, the Laogai.

BEST KEPT SECRET

The quality of a prisoner's labor output is seen as an indication of whether or not he has truly reformed. Each type of work and each prisoner has a daily quota which must be met; otherwise, there are various forms of punishment for one who is "not following directions" or has a "lazy labor attitude." Other measures used to compel prisoners to labor are revoking prisoners' writing or receiving letters rights, solitary confinement and torture. Prisoner food is rationed and can be reduced or cut off for any reason by the police. Food rations are kept at barely subsistence level, but there is always an expected level of production and output.

These Laogai enterprises are very profitable year after year since there are no labor costs and because production numbers are constantly monitored and increased. The production of the Laogai is definitely an integral part of the Chinese Communist's drive to modernize in its "socialist market economy." The Laogai is most definitely state-sanctioned slave labor. The scope of the Laogai, however, is more difficult to define. In the past forty-five years, there has never been any statement or report from the Communist Party, the legislative organs, or the Department of Statistics regarding the total number of people who have been sent to the Laogai or even how many of the three types of personnel are currently detained in these camps.

According to the Laogai Foundation's research, the number of arrested and sentenced convicted criminals currently in the Laogai is between four and six million. The number of prisoners who are officially not calculated but are detained in the detention centers, country and municipal jails, and secret military prisons is probably around one million.

In summary, the cumulative number of convicted Laogai and laojiao subjects confined in the Laogai system during the past forty-five years is conservatively around 50 million.

READING

2

BURMA: SLAVE NATION

John Pilger

*John Pilger (and film partner David Munro) are international journal-
ists. Posing as "exotic travel specialists," Pilger and partner brought the
camera inside Burma to record the testimony of the Burmese people.
In 1993, Pilger covered the tragic events in East Timor.*

■ **POINTS TO CONSIDER**

1. Why does Pilger describe Burma as a "prison without walls?"

2. Evaluate the situation in Burma and tell what strikes you as
   different about the regime in Burma.

3. Speculate about the lack of media coverage on Burma, and explain
   what leads you to your conclusions.

John Pilger, "A Cry for Freedom," **New Internationalist**, June 1996, 7-11 and "Slave
Nation," **New Internationalist,** June 1996, 12-13. Reprinted by permission, **New
Internationalist,** Toronto. Subscription (Canada) $38.50 (includes $2.94 GST) – individual 1 year, $64.20 (includes $4.20 GST) – $60.00 institution 1 year, 35 Riviera Drive,
Unit 17, Markham, ON L3R SN4, (905) 946-0407, (905) 946-0410 (fax), Magazine @
indas.on.can. Subscription (United States) $35.98 – individual 1 year, $60.00 – institution 1 year, PO Box 1143, Lewiston, NY 14092, (905) 946-0407, (905) 946-0410 (fax).

No modern state, whatever its totalitarian stripe, has turned itself into a vast slave labor camp in order to "develop." Milan Kundera once wrote that the "struggle of people against power is the struggle of memory against forgetting." Few outside Burma will know about the epic events here between 1988 and 1990. Few will have heard of the White Bridge on Inya Lake in the centre of Rangoon, now known to foreign business people as the site of an "international business centre." Yet it was here that an uprising as momentous as the storming of the Berlin Wall, 1989, was sparked. On 18 March, 1988, hundreds of schoolchildren and students marched along it, singing the national anthem. It was as joyful as it was defiant. When suddenly they saw behind them the steel helmets of the *Lon Htein,* the "riot police," and knew they were trapped...

SHOOT TO KILL

Unlike the bloody response to China's democracy movement in Tiananmen Square the following year, there were no TV cameras linked to satellite dishes when Ne Win kept his promise to "shoot to kill those who stand against us." As many as 10,000 died in the streets and in the prisons, under torture, and even in their homes as the army's feared Brengun-carriers stormed the crooked lanes, firing at random into flimsy homes. Anyone with a camera was a target. Perhaps the world only really took notice when a charismatic woman, Aung San Suu Kyi, daughter of the national hero Aung San, was placed under house-arrest in July 1989. Thereafter, so the generals calculated, they could proceed with an election that, without her, they were certain to win and which would legitimize their dictatorship. In fact, they lost spectacularly; Suu Kyi's National League for Democracy (NLD) won 82 per cent of the Parliamentary seats; she even swept the board in principal army cantonments.

A PRISON WITHOUT WALLS

Shocked, the generals (who had renamed the regime the State Law and Order Council, known by its Orwellian moniker SLORC) threw most of the newly elected Parliament into prison and turned Burma into what Amnesty has described as "a prison without walls." Since then, year upon year, the United Nations

16

Commission of Human Rights has translated Burma's tyranny into the following catalogue: "Torture, summary and arbitrary executions, forced labor, abuse of women, politically motivated arrests and detention, forced displacement, important restrictions on the freedoms of expression and association and oppression of ethnic and religious minorities..." One report that drew me to Burma was by Human Rights Watch which said that despite the release of Aung Sang Suu Kyi from house arrest, "the overall human-rights situation is worsening... As the SLORC has moved to attract international investment, at least two million people have been forced to work for no pay under brutal conditions to rebuild Burma's long-neglected infrastructure"...

Having opened Burma to the "free market" and released its most famous prisoner, the SLORC bargained that the rapacious instincts of the "Asian tiger" states and the venerable plunderers of the West would respond with the investment it craved...

SLAVE LABOR

Scheming despots are, of course, nothing new. What sets SLORC-run Burma apart is slave labor and massive displacement of whole sections of the population. No modern state, whatever its totalitarian stripe, has turned itself into a vast slave labor camp in order to "develop." Certainly, Pol Pot tried it as a means of control, but none matches the SLORC in paving its way to "the market" with such brutal audacity. This will attract capital and eventually loans will be granted by the World Bank and the International Monetary Fund (IMF); and "globalization" will mark another gain and humanity another loss...

The full force of these events struck me in the deep south of Burma, in Mon State, where David Munro and I found what has been described as the "second death railway." Connecting the towns of Ye and Tavoy, it is an extension of the notorious line built by the Japanese with the lives of more than 100,000 Asians and Allied prisoners of war. We came upon it in dense jungle beyond a village where emaciated young girls held out silver urns for contributions to the welfare of their community, a Buddhist tradition. Their face masks of *thanaka* – a yellow paste from tree-bark that protects and nourishes the skin – gave the appearance of small ghosts emerging from the undergrowth. They were fortunate compared with the gangs of children at work half a mile away.

NO ONE CAN ESCAPE

While adult slave workers toiled on 20-foot embankments, the children were engaged in a crude brickworks, most of them exposed to the pre-monsoon glare and heat. Their ages ranged from teens down to nine-year-olds. A ten-year-old boy was employed in a hole beneath a clay-mixer, turned by two yoked buffalo. His size was crucial; an adult would not be able to do his job, which was to catch the cement-like clay as it oozed out of the grinder in time to be collected in a barrow. There was an urgent rhythm about his movements: there had to be; if he faltered the clay would bury him. As we approached him a barrow-load fell sideways onto him, and I had to intervene to free him. One estimate is that, out of 200,000 adults and children forced to build the railway, up to 300 have died from exhaustion and disease or have been killed. This seems conservative. We counted some 20 bridges in the area, and children appeared to be working on all of them. "No one can escape forced labor," one villager told me. "SLORC officials or the army go from village to village. They take a child, as long as he is strong enough, without asking permissions of the parent"…

BURMESE CITIZEN INTERVIEWED BY JOHN PILGER

I was a government servant responsible for searching out coal mines for the Department of Geological Survey and Mineral Exploration, when I got a letter from my mother in December 1995. She wrote that she was unwell; she had cancer of the uterus and begged me to come back home to Tavoy in case she died…

I arrived home in late December and stayed there until March when I was ordered to do two weeks forced labor on the railroad. I had to bring enough food to provide for myself during this time. The work began at 6:00 a.m. and went on till evening. We had to get up at 4:00 and cook rice to take with us because the worksite was several miles away. Each day we had to cut 50 bamboo canes and 20 pillars.

There were also prisoners working with us on the site, and while we stopped to have our lunch they had to carry on working, pulling huge, heavy rollers in order to flatten the ground. Those prisoners worked like buffaloes. Sometimes the roller was so heavy it just wouldn't budge. Then the soldiers would beat the prisoners with huge canes, drawing blood. And the prisoners were

SLAVERY IN THE SUDAN

Slavery began in earnest under the previous government of Prime Minister Sadiq el Mahdi (1986-89), whose electoral credentials and pro-Western foreign policy muted human rights criticism while he was in office. Since then, Khartoum has used the very same militias that take slaves as important military allies in their war against rebels in the South...

The vast majority of Sudan's estimated several thousand slaves are members of the Dinka tribe living in the north of the Bahr el Ghazal region. Most were captured between 1985 and 1989 as a byproduct of raids by the militias. Relatively few have been taken since then, although the increase in militia raids since 1995 is an ominous augur.

Alex de Waal, "Sudan: Social Engineering, Slavery and War," **Covert Action Quarterly**, Spring 1997: 56-63.

---

not allowed to have a drop of water or a mouthful of food until it was time for them to have a meal. There were vendors who came to sell us food which only those with money could buy...

I came down with malaria and had to go to the health centre to buy some tablets. They helped me feel better, but the fever returned. When I went back to the health centre they refused to give me a day's medical leave and told me to get back to work. I did so, but I felt terrible. I could hardly stand and eventually I collapsed. Luckily, the supervisor was sympathetic and sent me back to the camp to rest...

BLOOD IN THE WATER

I completed my duty as a "voluntary servant" on the railroad and went home to Tavoy – only to be called by the area headman to serve as a porter. He said that one man per household had to serve. When I asked him whether, as a government servant, I should be required to serve as a porter he replied: "If you can't do it, I'll take your mother and your sisters." I was very upset by this, so I agreed to go.

I was sent to Myoma Police Station where I was locked up, together with all the other porters. There were 370 of us – from four townships – and that afternoon we were taken away in seven trucks… When we arrived at Yebyu we were again locked up and not given any food or water. We were not even allowed to go to the toilet…In the evening some soldiers' wives came to sell us noodles, snacks and bottles of alcohol…The people who were forced to work could not afford food, and many were starving.

Early the next morning we were sent to Sinma Camp. We had to carry heavy bundles on our backs and in our arms and had sacks tied to our heads…The terrain was rocky, and some people fell down into the valleys. Others became ill.

One old man accidentally dropped his rice sack into a small river. The soldiers thought he was trying to escape so they shot him in the head. I could see the blood coming out of his bullet wound, and the flow of the water was so fast that he was carried away by the river. Another man – over 60 years old – just couldn't carry his bag of rice any longer. He dropped it and as he did so his *longhi* (cloth wrapped round the waist) fell off. One of the captains pulled him up and beat him on the head with a huge cane. He was left with a gaping wound and forced to carry his sack again.

At the base of the Natyin Mountain the ground was being prepared for gas pipelines, and we were forced to stop here and do some of the work. On the third day four or five Englishmen came. We completed our work and continued on our way.

READING

3

MADE IN THE USA: SWEATSHOPS EXPLOIT IMMIGRANT WOMEN

William Branigin

William Branigin wrote the following for the Washington Post National Weekly. *He is a staff writer for the* Washington Post.

■ **POINTS TO CONSIDER**

1. From descriptions in the article, discuss the meaning of "sweat-shop."

2. How are sweatshops allowed to operate in the United States?

3. Describe the structure of the garment industry. Do retailers share some of the blame for the return of sweatshops? Explain.

Excerpted from William Branigin, "Sweatshops Are Back," **The Washington Post National Weekly Edition**. 24 February 1997: 6-7. © 1997 **The Washington Post**. Reprinted with permission.

Despite a ledger of laws against them, sweatshops have made a remarkable comeback in America, evolving from a relative anomaly into a commonplace, even indispensable, part of the U.S. garment industry.

After an arduous trek across the border from her native Mexico, Aurora Blancas made her way to New York City and took the first job she could find: sweeping floors and packaging clothes sewn by other illegal immigrants at a sweatshop in the garment district.

No experience – or documents – necessary. "I started working the same day I asked for the job," she says. "The boss asked me my name and how old I was. Nothing more." But unlike her fellow workers, Blancas, 28, did not accept quietly the exploitation and abuse that followed when she was hired to work in the dilapidated Eighth Avenue building. Although her willingness to speak out makes Blancas unusual, the place that employed her and the conditions she found there are not.

RETURN OF SWEATSHOPS

Despite a ledger of laws against them and periodic pledges by government and business leaders to crack down, sweatshops have made a remarkable comeback in America, evolving from a relative anomaly into a commonplace, even indispensable, part of the U.S. garment industry.

They have also evolved almost entirely into a phenomenon of immigrants. According to federal investigators and union officials, most such factories are owned by newcomers from Asia, who often exploit other immigrants, many of them illegal, either from Asia or Latin America. Typically, both the workers and the employers see themselves as victims of a system dominated by increasingly powerful major retailers.

In Blancas' case, the owner of the 14th-floor shop in which she worked is a South Korean immigrant whose clothes are sold to suppliers of such stores as Wal-Mart and Kmart. According to Blancas and another former worker, he refused to pay the minimum wage or overtime to his three dozen, mostly female employees. The workers typically toiled at their sewing machines and presses for up to 60 hours a week in a room with wires hanging from the ceiling, three small fans that served as the only source of ventilation and no fire exits. Wages, usually paid in cash to avoid taxes, often were arbitrarily cut or delayed if the owner ran short of funds. Employees who missed a day would be illegally "fined" $30, on top of losing a day's pay.

When workers made mistakes, the owner's wife would scream at them, throw garments in their faces and sometimes pull their hair or hit them. One newly arrived young woman was summarily fired for yawning on the job. After Blancas demanded higher wages and brought the sweatshop to the attention of a garment workers union, she was fired.

Whether operating openly in decrepit buildings in New York or Los Angeles or hidden away illegally in the people's homes in Dallas, sweatshops violate labor and tax laws amid cutthroat competition for orders that filter down from the retailers.

PROFITS UP, WAGES DOWN

The return of the kind of sweatshops that flourished early this century – and were thought to have been largely eliminated – reflects fundamental changes in the garment industry and, more broadly, in American society. The shops have become part of a vast underground economy, shielded by an overlay of laissez-faire practices and tacit accommodations.

Clothing designers and retailers depend on the sweatshops for fast delivery and big profit margins. Unions, hopeful of eventually organizing these workers, appear to be more interested in preserving manufacturing jobs than driving them out of business. Large pools of illegal immigrants are so anxious for work that they accept the shops' meager wages and are often too fearful to complain. Consumers keep gravitating toward the lowest prices they can find. And government agencies do not field enough investigators or cooperate sufficiently with each other to pursue the shops effectively and enforce the laws that would eradicate them.

Helping sweatshops to thrive have been technological advances that allow retailers to determine instantly what is selling and to order more of it. This allows stores to limit inventory and avoid getting stuck with large volumes of unpopular apparel. But it also requires quick turnaround, which favors domestic manufacturers. The pressures on these manufacturers to produce garments quickly and still compete with cheap foreign imports have tended to drive down wages and working conditions among the sewing shops that lie at the bottom of the industry.

Yet, there is no shortage of workers for these jobs because of a broader change in American society: increasing waves of legal and illegal immigration since the 1970s and growing concentrations of immigrants in cities such as Los Angeles and New York.

The sweatshops' revival also reflects a weakening of unions in the garment industry in recent years, in part because of their difficulties in trying to organize workers who are here illegally in the first place. For them, even a sub-minimum wage in the United States generally beats what they could earn in their homelands.

EMPLOYER ABUSE

Although the clandestine nature of much of the industry has made it hard to track, recent federal studies point to a rise in the number of U.S. sweatshops and a worsening of their conditions.

Union and Labor Department officials estimate that minimum wage and overtime violations, two of the basic parameters that define a sweatshop, prevail in more than half of the 22,000 U.S. sewing businesses. Many also pay their workers "off the books" to avoid various local, state and federal taxes.

The sweatshop conditions described by Blancas are "typical of the bottom of the industry," says Jeff Hermanson, director of the Garment Workers' Justice Center, a branch of the Union of Needletrades, Industrial and Textile Employees.

"Physical abuse is unfortunately quite common, and there's always the yelling," he says. The long hours, low wages and lack of benefits often found in Korean-owned sweatshops are also routine in shops run by Chinese and Latino owners, he says...

The Korean Apparel Manufacturers Association says it has been trying to get its 400 member companies in New York to pay at least the minimum wage. Most now do so, the group says. But these owners are themselves victims of punishing market forces, the group argues.

"The problem for the sewing companies is that the minimum wage goes higher and higher, and the price from manufacturers stays the same or goes down," says a spokeswoman for the Association who gave her name only as Hung. She acknowledges that some owners treat their workers harshly but says most do not. As for the illegal aliens among them, she concedes, "That's a problem."

24

"I'm looking for the union label."

For Blancas, trouble started almost immediately after she was hired by a shop called New Young Fashions. The owner, Kim Young Han, paid her less than the $160 a week she says she was promised. She worked six days a week, starting at 7:30 a.m. and finishing at 6 p.m. each weekday. Her pay averaged $2.54 an hour, according to figures compiled by the workers' center...

GARMENT INDUSTRY PYRAMID

Sweatshops such as Kim's lie at the bottom of what the Labor Department describes as a garment industry "food chain" beneath layers of suppliers, designers and middlemen, who compete fiercely for orders from the big retailers at the top.

It is a system that regulators and union officials say effectively insulates the big-name stores and fashion labels, allowing them to profess shock and ignorance of sweatshop conditions in which their clothes were sewn.

Major retailers, such as J.C. Penney, Sears and Wal-Mart, have quality-control inspectors who regularly visit work sites, and they know how much it costs to produce a garment at the minimum wage, a Labor Department official says. But under a 60-year-old law, the retailers can be held liable only if they had "direct knowledge" of labor violations involved in producing their goods.

The system also adds markups far in excess of the actual cost of the labor and material that went into the garments. Retailers say too many variables go into the final price of a garment to generalize about any of them, but Labor Department and union officials estimate that labor typically accounts for less than three percent of the U.S. retail price of clothing made in domestic sweatshops and as little as one-half of one percent for garments sewn abroad.

Because of the pressures weighing on those at the low end of the industry, shop owners such as Kim Young Han believe that they, too, are victims of the system. Sitting at his worn desk in a corner of the shop floor, Kim blames his problems on creditors, saying he is owed thousands of dollars by garment manufacturers who had subcontracted several large jobs to him. He produces letters to them demanding payment and threatening "legal action." All are written in longhand; he does not have a typewriter...

ENDING THE SLAVE SYSTEM

Shops at the bottom of the industry often go out of business, relocate and open under new names. Some fail altogether, never to reappear. But despite decades of lawmaking against them – and a public campaign by the Clinton administration following the 1995 exposure of a virtual slave-labor garment factory in Los Angeles – the system designed to eradicate the sweatshops has largely failed, union activists say.

Local, state and federal agencies charged with enforcing labor, immigration and tax laws have often failed to work together, allowing shop owners and workers to slip through the cracks of the system. Under a directive renewed by Mayor Rudolph W. Giuliani, a strong supporter of immigration, New York authorities are prohibited from sharing information with the Immigration and Naturalization Service (INS).

At the direction of the Administration and Congress, the INS has thrown the bulk of its resources at the southwestern border to prevent illegal immigrants from crossing into the United States from Mexico. Nationwide, only about 1,700 INS investigators are assigned to the interior of the country, and they spend less than 20 percent of their time enforcing immigration law at work sites of all kinds, according to the agency.

REGULATING CHILDREN

While government statistics do not track the number of working children, the Labor and Social Forecasting Secretariat estimates that various economic sectors employ a total of 800,000 workers under 14. Based on the 1990 census, the Public Education Secretariat guesses that more than 2.5 million kids between 6 and 14 don't attend school.

The second International Independent Tribunal Against Child Labor, held in Mexico City in March 1996, concluded that the economic forces behind expanded Mexican child labor were having the same effect in other countries. The number of working children globally has climbed to more than 250 million, according to the International Labor Organization. "Trade agreements like NAFTA and the General Agreement on Tariffs and Trade promised protections for workers," Investigator Lopez testified. "But they don't prohibit child labor, they regulate it..."

David Bacon, "NAFTA's Children," **Connection to the Americas**, May 1997: 3-6.

In a special effort in New York last year, INS agents arrested 1,824 illegal aliens during inspections of 150 work sites, most of them garment shops. However, because of a lack of detention space, almost all were released on their own recognizance and told to return for court hearings. "The percentage that shows up is minute," says Russ Bergeron, an INS spokesman. Most simply find another job in the underground economy, and many return to work at the same shops where they were arrested.

Ironically, labor groups such as the Garment Workers' Justice Center also play a part in keeping the sweatshops in business. Among the literature the Center distributes, for example, are fliers in English, Spanish and Korean that advise shop owners how to fend off searches by INS and Labor Department agents.

The fliers encourage employers to challenge inspections on grounds of discrimination and use legal stalling tactics that the INS says often enable them to fabricate employment eligibility records. Fliers in Spanish urge workers to "remain silent" when asked about their nationality, birthplace or entry into the United States.

The union says its main aim is to protect workers and preserve their jobs, regardless of their immigration status. When faced with labor violations, the Justice Center usually tries to work out a solution with the employer without government involvement.

Critics call the policy misguided. "If you're trying to defend a living standard, the minimum wage and Social Security and deal with legitimate companies," one independent labor activist argues, "helping these sweatshops exist would seem to be counterproductive".

THE LABOR OF CHILDREN

UNICEF

The United Nations Children's Fund (UNICEF) was created in 1947, as the arm of the United Nations in monitoring and acting upon the state of children globally. Each year, UNICEF releases its report on the "State of the World's Children."

■ **POINTS TO CONSIDER**

1. Define the purpose and some of the principles of the UN Convention on the Rights of the Child.

2. Summarize the characteristics which distinguish exploitive from legitimate child labor.

3. What is meant by "structural adjustment programs?" What have been the implications of these programs, according to UNICEF?

4. Discuss myths about child labor. What kind of work is actually occurring, where, and why? What may be some of the difficulties in answering these questions?

Excerpted from The State of the World's Children 1997, New York: Oxford University Press for UNICEF, 1997.

The most powerful force driving children into hazardous, debilitating labor is the exploitation of poverty.

Fifty years ago, in the aftermath of the most devastating war in history, UNICEF was created on 11 December 1946 to provide succor to children. Developing countries emerging from the colonial era invoked the same principle to demand that children be given specific attention in international cooperation.

RIGHTS OF THE CHILD

This conviction, expressed as the Convention on the Rights of the Child, entered into international law on 2 September 1990, nine months after the Convention's adoption by the United Nations General Assembly.

Those rights are comprehensive. The Convention defines children as people below the age of 18 (article 1) whose "best interests" must be taken into account in all situations (article 3). It protects children's right to survive and develop (article 6) to their full potential, and among its provisions are those affirming children's right to the highest attainable standard of health care (article 24), and to express views (article 12) and receive information (article 13). Children have a right to be registered immediately after birth and to have a name and nationality (article 7), a right to play (article 31) and a right to protection from all forms of sexual exploitation and sexual abuse (article 34).

CHILD LABOR

While the vast majority of working children are found in developing countries, children routinely work in all countries. In every country, rich and poor, it is the nature of the work children do that determines whether or not they are harmed by it – not the plain fact of their working.

A decade ago, UNICEF determined that child labor is exploitative if it involves:

• full-time work at too early an age;

• too many hours spent working;

• work that exerts undue physical, social or psychological stress;

• work and life on the streets in bad conditions;

• inadequate pay;

- too much responsibility;
- work that hampers access to education;
- work that undermines children's dignity and self-esteem, such as slavery or bonded labor and sexual exploitation;
- work that is detrimental to full social and psychological development.

Among the aspects of a child's development that can be endangered by work are:

- physical development – including overall health, coordination, strength, vision and hearing;
- cognitive development – including literacy, numeracy and the acquisition of knowledge necessary to normal life;
- emotional development – including adequate self-esteem, family attachment, feelings of love and acceptance;
- social and moral development – including a sense of group identity, the ability to cooperate with others and the capacity to distinguish right from wrong.

Education helps a child develop cognitively, emotionally and socially, and it is an area often gravely jeopardized by child labor. Work can interfere with education in the following ways:

- it frequently absorbs so much time that school attendance is impossible;
- it often leaves children so exhausted that they lack the energy to attend school or cannot study effectively when in class;
- some occupations, especially seasonal agricultural work, cause children to miss too many days of class even though they are enrolled in school;
- the social environment of work sometimes undermines the value children place on education, something to which street children are particularly vulnerable;
- children mistreated in the workplace may be so traumatized that they cannot concentrate on school work or are rejected by teachers as disruptive.

WORKING CHILDREN

Worldwide, the big picture looks something like this: the vast majority of all child laborers live in Asia, Africa and Latin

America. Half of them can be found in Asia alone, although their proportion may be declining in Southeast Asia as per capita income increases, basic education spreads and family size decreases. Africa has an average of one in three children working. In Latin America, one child in five works. These proportions have increased partly due to the economic crisis of the 1980s and, in Africa, because of the lack of public investment in education as well as because of armed conflict. In both Africa and Latin America, only a tiny proportion of child workers are involved in the formal sector. The vast majority work for their families, in homes, in the fields and on the streets.

Child labor has increased substantially in Central and Eastern European countries as a result of the abrupt switch from centrally planned to market economies. In industrialized countries, such as the UK and the US, meanwhile, the growth of the service sector and the quest for a more flexible workforce have contributed to an expansion of child labor. Political unrest and HIV/AIDS in African countries have resulted in increased reliance on child labor.

POVERTY, EDUCATION, TRADITION

The most powerful force driving children into hazardous, debilitating labor is the exploitation of poverty. Where society is characterized by poverty and inequity, the incidence of child labor is likely to increase, as does the risk that it is exploitative.

The 1980s marked a serious downturn in the fortunes of many developing countries, as government indebtedness, unwise internal economic policies and recession resulted in economic crisis. The World Bank and the International Monetary Fund (IMF) responded by imposing on indebted nations, in return for loan guarantees, a package of policy prescriptions known as "structural adjustment programs." These sweeping economic reforms aimed to orient countries toward the needs of the global economy, promoting export crops and offering incentives to foreign investors while at the same time slashing government expenditure. All too often, the cuts in expenditure fell on health and education, on food subsidies and on social services, all needed most by the poor.

Cuts in social spending have hit education – the most important single step in ending child labor – particularly hard. The economic forces that propel children into hazardous work may be the

In cottage industries throughout the world, all family members contribute. In Honduras, a young boy sleeps at the work table where he stitches softballs in his home.

most powerful of all. But traditions and entrenched social patterns play a part, too.

Understanding all the various cultural factors that lead children into work is essential. But deference to tradition is often cited as a reason for not acting against intolerable forms of child labor. Children have an absolute, unnegotiable right to freedom from hazardous child labor – a right now established in international law.

DOMESTIC SERVICE

Child domestic workers are the world's most forgotten children, which is why it is worth considering their plight before that of other, more familiar groups of child workers. Although domestic service need not be hazardous, most of the time it is just that. Children in domestic servitude may well be the most vulnerable and exploited children of all, as well as the most difficult to protect. They are often extremely poorly paid or not paid at all; their terms and conditions are very often entirely at the whim of the employers and take no account of their legal rights; they are deprived of schooling, play and social activity, and of emotional support from family and friends. They are vulnerable to physical and sexual abuse.

FORCED AND BONDED LABOR

Many of the forms of child labor practiced around the world are "forced" in the sense that children are taught to accept the conditions of their lives and not to challenge them. But the situation of some children goes far beyond the acceptance of poor conditions. They find themselves in effective slavery. In South Asia, this has taken on a quasi-institutional form known as "bonded" child labor. Under this system, children, often only eight or nine years old, are pledged by their parents to factory owners or their agents in exchange for small loans. Their lifelong servitude never succeeds in even reducing the debt.

COMMERCIAL SEXUAL EXPLOITATION

The underground nature of the multi-billion-dollar illegal industry in the commercial sexual exploitation of children makes it difficult to gather reliable data. But non-governmental organizations (NGOs) in the field estimate that each year at least one million girls worldwide are lured or forced into this form of hazardous labor, which can verge on slavery. Boys are also often exploited.

INDUSTRIAL WORK

All over the world, children work in hazardous conditions. The industries are manifold, from leather-working in the Naples region of Italy to the pre-industrial brick-making of Colombia and Peru, which can involve children as young as eight.

STREET WORK

In contrast with child domestic workers, some children work in the most visible places possible – on the streets of developing world cities and towns. They are everywhere: hawking in markets and darting in and out of traffic jams, plying their trade at bus and train stations, in front of hotels and shopping malls. They share the streets with millions of adults, many of whom regard them as nuisances, if not as dangerous mini-criminals. What most of these children actually do on the streets is, of course, work. The street is a cruel and hazardous workplace, often jeopardizing even children's lives. They can be murdered by organized crime, by other young people or even by the police.

GIRLS' WORK

Most of the hazards faced by boy laborers are faced by girls, too. Yet girls have extra problems of their own: from the sexual pressures of employers to exclusion from education. No strategy to combat child labor can begin to be successful unless these special dangers facing girls are systematically taken into account.

In virtually every area of life and in every country, as these annual State of the World's Children Reports have long noted, girls and women routinely bear burdens and endure treatment that reflect their unequal status. So it is with child labor. Working girls are often invisible, treated as if they did not exist.

The gender gap becomes a vicious circle for girls all over the developing world. Unable to attend school because of their low social status or their domestic responsibilities, they are denied the extra power and wider horizons that education would bring. If they seek work outside the home, their opportunities are limited to the most menial tasks. Their low status is reinforced and passed on to the next generation.

WOMEN SLAVES OF THE SEX TRADE

Alice Leuchtag

Alice Leuchtag is an activist for women's liberation. The following piece appeared in The Humanist. The Humanist *is a publication of the American Humanist Association which describes humanism as "a naturalistic and democratic outlook, informed by science, inspired by art, and motivated by compassion to broad areas of social and personal concern."*

■ **POINTS TO CONSIDER**

1. Define the terms "international prostitution" and "sex tour industry."

2. Describe the link between rural poverty and urban prostitution.

3. Evaluate the position of the First World in the proliferation of Third World prostitution. For example, comment on the effects of international development programs, according to the author.

4. Why does the author criticize and praise the policies of the Filipino government in their efforts to eliminate prostitution?

5. How does war affect prostitution?

Alice Leuchtag, "Merchants of Flesh: International Prostitution and the War on Women's Rights," **The Humanist**, March/Apr. 1995: 11-16. Reprinted with permission of the author.

The supply side of international organized prostitution requires girls, young women, and families in Third World countries to be economically desperate, uneducated, and with few options.

Internationally organized prostitution depends on a pernicious combination of Third World poverty, First World economic development policies, laws that permit international trafficking and indentured servitude, and worldwide patriarchal cultural norms that encourage male sexual prerogatives. But despite the sheer magnitude of these factors, there are some signs of hope. More and more women, both in the Third World and the developed world, are discussing the global politics of prostitution: the direct links between developmental policies pushed by the World Bank and the International Monetary Fund and the experiences of 14- and 15-year-old village girls in such countries as Kenya, India, Nepal, Bangladesh, Thailand, the Philippines, Brazil, and Honduras. In some places, activists are organizing to help the children and women who have been forced into a life of prostitution. And feminists and others are beginning to demand an end to those policies, laws, and practices which promote prostitution as a multinational growth industry.

Each year thousands of uneducated, orphaned, abandoned, and destitute girls and young women across Asia, the Pacific, and Africa are given false promises of good jobs, transported across borders, and then sold into brothels in urban centers from Bombay to Bangkok to Nairobi. A 1991 conference of Southeast Asian women's organizations estimated that 30 million women had been sold worldwide since the mid-1970s. Traffickers scour train stations, poor villages, and urban streets looking for young girls and women who appear vulnerable. In 1991, the Human Rights Commission of Pakistan estimated that there were 200,000 Bangladeshi women in forced prostitution in Pakistan, yet not a single trafficker was arrested or convicted that year. When arrests do occur, it is always the women who are arrested and charged with violation of immigration laws.

New Delhi has become a major center in South Asia for the international buying and selling of girls and women. In Bombay, there are at least 100,000 prostitutes in 25 grubby red-light districts. Many were lured into the city by promises of domestic or factory jobs or marriage. The women (some actually girls as young as 11) learn too late that they are being sold into prostitution. Shamed by their fate, frightened, and financially indebted to the brothel owners for their food and clothes, few can escape their circumstances; and even if they do, it is unlikely they will be accepted back into their villages because their families often come to depend upon the money sent home from their meager earnings (after the brothel has taken at least 50 percent)...

The fate of these women is dismal. In Bombay, more than one-third of all prostitutes tested positive for HIV, making them, according to the World Health Organization, one of the highest risk groups in the world...

THE PACKAGED SEX TOUR

A growing form of international prostitution is the government-sponsored sex tour. Thailand is a notorious example. In bars all along Bangkok's Pat Bong and Soi Cow-boy streets, teenage girls, just brought in from rural villages where female modesty is a strong part of Thai culture, dance awkwardly on stage in scanty bathing suits with numbers pinned on. Waitresses circulate among the tables taking drink and girl orders. In a brothel in Chiang Mai, young women sit behind a plate-glass display window. Each wears a heart-shaped price tag on her blouse advertising how much a half hour of sex with her will cost. The women are always on call, with 10 to 20 customers a day. In this particular brothel, four out of five women carry the AIDS virus. Even in the more expensive brothels, at least one out of five women is infected.

Despite these ominous facts, the brothels and bars of Bangkok and other Thai cities are described in glowing, exotic terms by Thai government literature. It is all part of the promotion of tourism among businessmen from Japan, Germany, Norway, Saudi Arabia, Holland, Australia, and the United States. Foreign johns, who feel safely anonymous away from home, are now among Thailand's leading sources of hard currency. In 1991, a group of women from several countries, including the United States, picketed the World Trade Fair in Tokyo to protest Thailand's government-sponsored exploitation of girls and women.

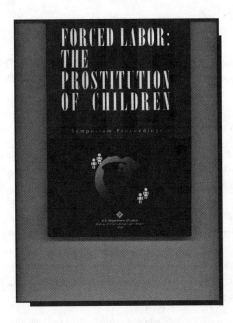

Papers from a symposium co-sponsored by the U.S. Department of Labor, Bureau of International Affairs, the Women's Bureau, and the U.S. Department of State, Bureau of Democracy, Human Rights and Labor, held on September 29, 1995 at the U.S. Department of Labor in Washington, DC.

Thailand's sex tour industry is best understood from a global economic perspective. In 1967, Thailand contracted with the U.S. government to provide "rest and recreation" services to the troops during the Vietnam War. Robert McNamara was then U.S. Secretary of Defense. In 1971, while the War was still on, the World Bank, headed by the same Robert McNamara, recommended the development of mass tourism in Thailand as a way for the country to pay on its debts to the Bank for agricultural development loans. The economic initiatives started by the Bank's report led directly to the $4-billion-a-year multi-national Thai sex tour industry, which involves a network of cozy relations between banks, airlines, tour operators, hotels, and bar and brothel owners and agents, all of whom extract their profits from the bodies of pitifully underpaid village girls, some as young as 14...

Compared to the magnitude of organized prostitution in Thailand, organized resistance is still on a much smaller scale. Organizations such as Friends of Women and Empower work with prostitutes, teaching them about condoms and about AIDS and other risks that they face. Empower enrolls over 100 women in English classes so they can avoid being cheated by foreign johns. Chantawipa Apisuk, who runs Empower, says, "People don't want to talk about the profiteers." Apisuk maintains that the rich need to be controlled, not the poor, and she asks, "Why not open factories instead of brothels and bars?" However, the terrible fire at a doll factory near Bangkok in 1993 gives an idea of the current conditions of employment options outside the sex industry for young, uneducated Thai women.

INDENTURED SERVITUDE

Most of the women in city brothels come from small rural villages where agricultural development policies have pushed many families off the land and into poverty. Slick brothel agents visit the villages where they induce parents to bond their daughters to the brothels in exchange for cash, supposedly an advance on salary. Additional inducements – such as refrigerators, television sets, or jewelry – may be offered, especially for virgins under age 17. Brothel agents may induce village monks to hold beauty contests on temple grounds so that parents will be more willing to bring their daughters to market.

Once in a brothel, a young woman is virtually in indentured servitude. She must earn back her "debt." She must buy from the company store at inflated prices, while money is deducted for days lost due to illness, menstruation, turning away a customer who refuses to wear a condom, or any of many "sins." She may never see any of the money she earns but may work her entire time trying to pay off her debt. Thai brothels are nationwide chains, and women are shipped around the country. If a woman becomes infected with the AIDs virus or becomes pregnant, she may be sent home with nothing but bus fare. At home, her future is bleak, with small chance of being accepted back by her family. It is likely she will end her days in a village brothel.

Organized prostitution and the sex tour business have spread to Cambodia, South Korea, and Myanmar (formerly Burma). Cambodian women activists and the Cambodian Human Rights Task Force report that forced prostitution is growing and that the male-dominated government does nothing about it...

THE NATION'S DIGNITY

In the Philippines (as in Thailand), international banks encouraged the government to promote tourism as the primary method of economic development. Filipino women were seen as a natural resource to be exploited. By the mid-1980s, sex tourism had

BILLION DOLLAR INDUSTRY

According to a recent study by the International Commission of Jurists, the sex market for minors under 16 is a $5 billion industry including agents, madams, pimps and criminal organizations. It is an industry driven by poverty, greed and a callous demand for sex.

Laura J. Lederer, "Poor Children Targets of Sex Exploitation," **National Catholic Reporter**, November 22, 1996: 11.

become pivotal to the government's economic survival. Women's activist groups, such as Gabriela, urged Corazon Aquino, who campaigned on a pledge to restore the nation's dignity after long years of the Marcos dictatorship, to give up sex tourism as a development strategy. They also urged her not to renew leases on the two U.S. military bases, around which prostitution had grown along with many acts of violence by U.S. servicemen against Filipinas. In their campaign against the bases, the activists were ultimately successful – perhaps helped along by the eruption of the volcano, Mt. Pinatubo.

Aquino, though not a feminist, did change the leadership of the tourism ministry and some of its policies. But when, without consulting women's groups, she authorized raids on the bars and massage parlors in Ermita (the red-light district of Manila), feminists were alarmed. Hardly any pimps, brothel owners, bar and hotel owners, or johns were arrested. Yet hundreds of women were arrested, and the government did nothing to provide alternative jobs or education. Not until 1988, when Miriam Defensor Santiago became the Philippines Commissioner of Immigration, did the government take any significant action; shortly thereafter, some American, German, Australian, Belgian, British, Canadian, Dutch, Japanese, Swiss, and Spanish johns who purchased sex with children were deported. In 1993, a new law was passed in the Philippines under which pimps and johns now face prison and deportation...

PUTTING IT IN PERSPECTIVE

The supply side of international organized prostitution requires girls, young women, and families in Third World countries to be economically desperate, uneducated, and with few options. This desperation has frequently been brought about or exacerbated by development policies that have cut back on social services and have pushed rural families off their land. There must also be a virtual army of recruiters, brokers, and traffickers who are able to operate within and between countries with relative impunity and who have at their command a variety of methods to obtain these economically desperate girls and women. Finally, there is a system of indentured servitude so that, once a girl or young woman finds herself in the sex trade, it is difficult to leave...

READING

6

THE INVISIBLE SOLDIERS: CHILD COMBATANTS

The Center for Defense Information

The Center for Defense Information is a Washington, D.C., based, nonprofit organization, which promotes effective defense and exposes wasteful, ineffective or immoral practices of war and defense build-up. Founded by retired military officers, CDI has been promoting appropriate defense policy for 25 years. The following article appeared in their newsletter, The Defense Monitor.

■ POINTS TO CONSIDER

1. Define the term "invisible soldier."

2. Evaluate the claim that voluntary service of children is misleading.

3. According to the article, describe the scope or extent of the problem of child combatants.

4. Why are both the employment and deactivation of child soldiers disturbing, according to the authors?

5. Summarize the body of national and international law concerning child soldiers.

"The Invisible Soldiers: Child Combatants," **The Defense Monitor,** Vol. XXVI, No. 4, July 1997. **The Defense Monitor** is sent without charge to donors of $35.00 or more to The Center for Defense Information, 1500 Massachusetts Ave., NW, Washington, D.C. 20005, (202) 862-0700, fax (202) 862-0708, info@cdi.org.

This phenomenon of child soldiers is both new and horrifying.

Sadly, the "role of innocents" has been increasingly ignored over the past several decades as civilians are more affected by war and targeted by various factions. In recent decades the proportion of war victims who are civilians has leapt dramatically from five percent to over 90 percent.

CHILDREN AS COMBATANTS

Worst of all, children are increasingly being used as combatants...According to the most recent annual human rights report of the U.S. State Department, "an estimated quarter of a million children, even as young as age five, have been conscripted to serve as soldiers in dozens of armed conflicts around the world, some with armed insurgencies, such as the Khmer Rouge, the Shining Path of Peru, and Palestinian groups in Lebanon, and some in regular armies, such as those of Cambodia, Uganda, Angola, and Sudan."

This phenomenon of child soldiers is both new and horrifying. It violates the universal rule that children simply have no part in warfare. It also shows the alarming state of morals around the world. This was noted in an important study released by the United Nations last year. The report "Impact of Armed Conflict on Children," noted that "more and more of the world is being sucked into a space in which children are slaughtered, raped, and maimed; a space in which children are exploited as soldiers; a space in which children are starved and exposed to extreme brutality. Such unregulated terror and violence speak of deliberate victimization. There are few further depths to which humanity can sink."

Yet in spite of this and other reports the issue of child soldiers is still largely an invisible one. A recent study by the Swedish group Rädda Barnen (Save the Children) concludes that those who employ children as soldiers, deny their existence. No record is kept of their numbers or ages, and ages are falsified. Many are not part of the formally claimed strength of the forces or groups to which they are attached, but they are unacknowledged members.

INVISIBLE SOLDIERS

They are invisible because most spend their time in remote conflict zones away from both public view and media scrutiny. They are invisible because they simply vanish. They never return from the battlefield because they are killed or, having been injured, are tragically abandoned. Lastly, those in their early teens are invisible because they are less obviously children. And in a larger sense, perhaps this is the greatest tragedy. Individually they all grow older. The very fact that the soldier survives means the child disappears. The child in the soldier becomes invisible, locked inside an "adult" soldier or an "adult" former soldier.

Involving children as soldiers has been made easier by the proliferation of inexpensive light weapons. As recently as a generation ago battlefield weapons were still heavy and bulky, generally limiting children's participation to support roles. But modern guns are so light that children can easily use them and so simple that they can be stripped and reassembled by a child of 10. The unrestrained international arms trade in conventional arms has made assault rifles such as the AK-47 cheap and widely available. The poorest communities now have access to weapons capable of transforming any local conflict into bloody slaughter.

RECRUITING CHILD SOLDIERS

Armed conflict itself contributes to the increasing number of child soldiers. War disrupts normal economic and social conditions and causes educational opportunities to shrink or disappear. Under these circumstances, recruits tend to get younger and younger...

Quite often child "recruits" are arbitrarily seized from the streets or even from schools and orphanages...In addition to being forcibly recruited, children also voluntarily present themselves for service. It is misleading, however, to consider this "voluntary." They may be driven by cultural, social, political or, more often, economic pressures. Hunger and poverty often drive parents to offer their children for service. In some cases, armies pay a minor wage directly to the family. Children themselves may volunteer if they believe that this is the only way to obtain regular meals, clothing, or medical attention. Some parents encourage their daughters to become soldiers if their marriage prospects are poor.

Too often, parents may even see material advantages in having their children involved and are reluctant to forego the benefits that child combatants obtain for their families...Sometimes, the structural conditions in a country induce children to become soldiers.

Many children have personally experienced or witnessed extremes of physical violence, including summary executions, death squad killings, disappearances, torture, arrest or detention, sexual abuse, bombings, forced displacement, destruction of home or property, and massacres. Revenge can be a particularly strong motivation to "join up."

HOW CHILD SOLDIERS ARE USED

In late 1996 children below 18 years of age were reportedly participating in 33 ongoing or recently ended conflicts, according to Rädda Barnen. In 26 of the conflicts, almost 80%, the children involved were under 15, the current minimum age limit stipulated in international law for participation in hostilities...

Countries where children serve in government forces include Burma, Cambodia, Colombia, Guatemala, Peru, and Sudan. Among opposition groups known to use children are the Khmer Rouge in Cambodia, the PKK in Turkey, the LTTE in Sri Lanka, and the LRA in Uganda. Although public awareness of child soldiers is relatively new, their use in some countries is a long-standing practice. In Cambodia, for example, the existence of child soldiers has been acknowledged for 25 years. Nevertheless, the scale of the problem has been growing substantially in recent years.

Once recruited as soldiers, children generally receive much the same treatment as adults, including often brutal induction cere-monies. The impact of the regular use of physical and emotional abuse involving degradation and humiliation of younger recruits to "indoctrinate" discipline and induce fear of superiors usually results in low self-esteem, guilt feelings, and violent solutions to problems...

Although the majority of child soldiers are boys, armed groups also recruit girls, many of whom perform the same functions as boys. Girls may also be forced to provide sexual services...Treatment of captured child soldiers by government forces is often brutal. Many are treated the same as captured adult soldiers. They are considered to be criminals or terrorists and held in military prisons. Many captured child soldiers of both sexes are subjected to abusive interrogation procedures, torture, isolation, rape, and death threats...

Among the rights guaranteed by the Convention on the Rights of the Child is the right to play. A boy on a rope swing in Barbados, where the Convention was ratifed in 1990.

CONSEQUENCES

Physical injury carries additional emotional, psychological, economic, and social disadvantages. Loss of sight or hearing are severe obstacles to educational or social development. Loss of limbs may require repeated amputations for those still growing since the bone of the amputated limb grows more than the surrounding tissue. They will also require new prostheses frequently. In addition to the trauma, treatment costs may be too high or the necessary facilities may be unavailable. In Mozambique demobilized child soldiers complain of health problems related to bullets and shrapnel still lodged in their bodies. Many families do not have the resources to pay for operations to remove these objects. In societies with high levels of unemployment, the additional disadvantages from wounds may be too hard to overcome.

Perhaps the most severe long-term consequences of children serving as soldiers may be on their moral development. When the fighting ends and children return to society, it is very difficult to place them in the more sedate surroundings of schools or families. Their moral system is dominated by fear of violence from whomever is superior in the hierarchy. Child soldiers find it difficult to disengage from the idea that violence is a legitimate means

47

of achieving one's aims, and find the transition to a nonviolent life-style difficult.

How can they learn from unarmed adults? How can they work? How can they marry and rear children? How can they be expected to be functioning members of a civil society when their entire formative experience is that society is organized around fear of violence?…

But, given the numerous wars around the world and the lack of resources to ameliorate their effects in the countries where they take place, these obligations are seldom honored. The proof of this is the fact that no peace treaty to date has formally recognized the existence of child combatants. As a result, their special needs are rarely if ever taken into account in demobilization programs.

But if simple human decency does not compel governments to care for children, pragmatic considerations of self-interest should. If children who were soldiers are not reintegrated into a post-conflict society, they may well contribute to future conflicts…

INTERNATIONAL LAW

The first international regulation dealing with the issue of children in armed conflict, the 1977 Additional Protocols to the Geneva Conventions, established a minimum age for recruitment. In 1986 international attention was dramatically focused on child soldiers in their modern form when Yoweri Museveni's National Resistance Army fought its way into Kampala, the capital of Uganda. Observers were stunned to see four- and five-year-olds in its ranks.

Although slow, the world finally reacted. In the UN Declaration of the Rights of the Child, adopted in 1989, the bearing of arms in battle is prohibited below age 15. Also in 1989 the UN General Assembly adopted the Convention on the Rights of the Child (CRC), the most rapidly and widely adopted human rights treaty in history. There are one hundred ninety signatories to the convention. The United States signed the CRC on February 16, 1995, but it has not ratified it. The only other country which has not ratified it is Somalia, which currently has no internationally recognized government.

Article 38 of the Treaty states, in part, that "Parties shall refrain from recruiting any person who has not attained the age of 15 years into their armed forces. In recruiting among those persons

LAND MINES

Land mines have been used in most conflicts since the end of the Second World War, especially in internal conflicts. These small, lethal weapons have indiscriminate effects and are triggered by innocent passersby, many of them children. Land mines are the most insidious of the light weapons that cause suffering to millions of children caught up in armed conflicts...

Mine victims are concentrated among the poorest of a society, people whose livelihood depends on herding animals, gathering firewood and cultivating fields. Child soldiers are particularly vulnerable as they are often used to explore known mine fields. In Cambodia, a survey of mine victims in military hospitals disclosed that 43 percent had been recruited as soldiers between the ages of 10 and 16.

Mary Evelyn Jegen, "Casualties of Warfare: Children and Childhood," **National Catholic Reporter**, Feb. 14, 1997: 12-13.

who have attained the age of 15 years but who have not attained the age of 18 years, States Parties shall endeavor to give priority to the oldest."

This language suggests that a compromise (not a very good one) was required. It is well known that at the time of the drafting of the Convention, the question of the minimum age of recruitment into the armed forces caused much controversy. Many wished to see the minimum age at 18 years in line with the general age of majority stated in Article 1 of the Conventions. In fact, Article 38 is the only provision in the Treaty which specifies that an age lower than 18 is acceptable.

Another questionable compromise is that Article 38 requires States to take all feasible measures to prevent only the child's direct participation in hostilities. This emphasis on "direct participation" actually lowers the standard of protection afforded by other international humanitarian laws, such as Additional Protocol II to the Geneva Conventions. The United States bears significant responsibility for this situation because at the time Article 38 was being drafted the U.S. delegate opposed using language which would make this as strong as other humanitarian law. He asserted that adopting the higher standard might even oblige an invaded United States to renounce self-defense! The inanity of this assertion is immediately obvious when one considers that the United States itself requires parental consent for volunteers under 18 to serve in the armed forces and does not assign those under 18 to combat duty...

SETTING STANDARDS

International law should recognize 18 years as the minimum age for recruitment (compulsory or voluntary) into any kind of armed forces and armed groups and for any kind of participation in hostilities. All governments and armed opposition groups who currently have persons under 18 years of age should be urged to demobilize them immediately. The United States should ratify the CRC and adopt a protocol making 18 years the minimum age for participation in hostilities.

WHAT IS EDITORIAL BIAS?

This activity may be used as an individualized study guide for students in libraries and resource centers or as a discussion catalyst in small group and classroom discussions.

The capacity to recognize an author's point of view is an essential reading skill. The skill to read with insight and understanding involves the ability to detect different kinds of opinions or bias. **Sex bias, race bias, ethnocentric bias, political bias,** and **religious bias** are five basic kinds of opinions expressed in editorials and all literature that attempts to persuade. They are briefly defined below.

Five Kinds of Editorial Opinion or Bias

Sex Bias — The expression of dislike for and/or feeling of superiority over the opposite sex or a particular sexual minority.

Race Bias — The expression of dislike for and/or feeling of superiority over a racial group.

Ethnocentric Bias — The expression of a belief that one's own group, race, religion, culture, or nation is superior. Ethnocentric persons judge others by their own standards and values.

Political Bias — The expression of political opinions and attitudes about domestic or foreign affairs.

Religious Bias — The expression of a religious belief or attitude.

Guidelines

1. From the readings in Chapter One, locate five sentences that provide examples of editorial opinion or bias.

2. Write down each of the above sentences and determine what kind of bias each sentence represents. Is it sex bias, race bias, ethnocentric bias, political bias, or religious bias?

3. Make up a one-sentence statement that would be an example of each of the following: sex bias, race bias, ethnocentric bias, political bias, and religious bias.

4. See if you can locate five sentences that are factual statements from the readings in Chapter One.

CHAPTER 2

SLAVE LABOR, CHILD LABOR, AND THE MAQUILADORES

7. THE SLAVES WE RENT   54
    A.V. Krebs

8. AMERICANS WON'T DO THE WORK   62
    James S. Holt

9. STOLEN YOUTH – DEGRADED CHILDREN   69
    Robert Weissman

10. BLANKET CONDEMNATION HELPS NO ONE   77
    Chris Brazier

11. SWEATSHOPS FOR THE WORLD'S POOR   84
    Joyce Bowers

12. OPPORTUNITY SHOPS FOR THE DISPOSSESSED   89
    Hans F. Sennholz

13. RETAILERS' RACE TO THE BOTTOM   94
    Charles Kernaghan

14. RETAILERS' OPPOSITION TO EXPLOITATION   101
    Robert Hall and Kathie Lee Gifford

15. END CHILD LABOR: BAN THEIR PRODUCTS   107
    Christopher H. Smith

16. END CHILD LABOR: BUY THEIR PRODUCTS   111
    William Anderson

    INTERPRETING EDITORIAL CARTOONS   116
    Reasoning Skill Activity

7

THE SLAVES WE RENT

A.V. Krebs

A.V. Krebs is director of the Corporate Agribusiness Research Project. He is the author of The Corporate Reapers: The Book of Agribusiness *(Essential Books: 1992).*

■ **POINTS TO CONSIDER**

1. Summarize the "history lessons" proposed by Krebs.

2. Why does the author make specific mention of California Governor Pete Wilson?

3. Explain the agribusiness connection to illegal immigration.

A.V. Krebs, "Immigrants: Agribusiness' Dirty Secret," **Progressive Populist**, May 1996: 5-6. Reprinted by permission.

Agribusiness both exploits and blames immigrant workers for many of the social ills which pervade our society.

Lost amidst the 1996 Presidential campaign rhetoric and the political posturing in Congress is the fact that the illegal immigration issue has historically been and remains even today agribusiness' dirty little secret.

From the blueberry fields of Maine to the poultry processing plants of the Delmarva region on the Mid-Atlantic Coast, from the tobacco fields of North Carolina to the corn fields of Iowa, from the kill floors of the beef packing plants of Nebraska, to the fruit and vegetable fields of California's fertile valleys, immigrants – the vast majority of them believed to be illegal – have and continue to supply agribusiness with cheap, docile, unorganized labor.

In addition, agribusiness in its single-minded pursuit of such labor, particularly in the U.S. Southwest, has historically instigated, encouraged and sanctioned such immigration.

ILLEGAL IMMIGRANTS

Paradoxically, when politicians and social commentators today discuss the "immigration crisis" it is almost always in terms of the Mexican border, with scant attention paid to those thousands of legal and illegal immigrants coming into the United States from other parts of the world.

For the moment, however, let's put aside the question of who really are "illegal" immigrants on territory that now comprises one third of the U.S. land mass and which once in fact belonged to Mexico prior to the Treaty of Guadalupe Hidalgo of 1848.

Here was land literally stolen from the Mexican people by a handful of thievish land barons in what land reformer Henry George once described as "a history of greed, of perjury, of corruption, of spoliation and high-handed robbery for which it will be difficult to find a parallel."

The long-term consequences of such action was that, in the words of Ernesto Galarza, author of the classic *Merchants of Labor*, the Treaty left "the toilers on one side of the border, the capital and the best land on the other."

Therefore, it is no accident that throughout U.S. history the chronic areas of rural poverty have remained the South, where the plantation system has dominated the agricultural scene, and the Southwest, where vast tracts of productive land have remained in the hands of a privileged few through the years.

Clearly, U.S. agribusiness can say of illegal immigrants that they are the "slaves we rent." When G.C. Hanna of the Department of Vegetable Crops, University of California-Davis, explained why he had undertaken the development of a tomato for processing and canning that could be harvested by a machine, he observed:

"I had gotten interested in the history of asparagus in California and I found that the first asparagus cutters were Chinese and the second group was Japanese. Then we had immigrating Italians and Portuguese, then the Hindus and then the Filipinos in the 1940s. And then I got to looking at the rest of our agricultural labor and I found out that most were imported nationalities and we were running out of nationalities to import."

NOT-SO-WELCOME GUESTS

A recent example of the hypocrisy that has surrounded the influx of "illegals," now publicly being decried in Congress and in our statehouses, is the current legislative effort to grant "temporary" visas to some 250,000 foreign farm workers.

This so-called "guest worker" program is but one more effort by corporate agribusiness to revive what three decades ago was called the *bracero* program which allowed over four million Mexican contract workers into the U.S. from 1942 to 1964 as part of a World War II "emergency" work program.

Such an attempt to revive the "guest worker" program was made unsuccessfully in 1984 in a bill co-sponsored by then-U.S. Senator Pete Wilson of California. In 1986 Wilson would also champion immigration legislation which facilitated a continuing supply of more than a million inexpensive farm laborers.

It should be no surprise, therefore, in light of this vast, cheap labor pool available to agribusiness, that Wilson as a U.S. Senator, according to the National Library on Money in Politics, received some $357,734 from agribusiness-oriented political action committees.

Although Wilson argued that his provision "would guarantee decent housing, workmen's compensation, and other benefits for

the seasonal farm worker," U.S. Labor Dept. statistics show that more than one million farm workers and their families already live below the poverty line, three-quarters of them receiving no government assistance. Two-thirds of all migrant farm workers, and fully one-half of settled farm workers, now earn poverty-level incomes.

Consequent to Wilson's 1986 legislation, immigration officials have estimated that between 30-70% of foreign farm workers in the U.S. obtained their jobs using fraudulent documents. At the same time the U.S. Labor Department has estimated that at any given time, 12%, or at least 190,000 domestic farm workers, are out of a job.

POLICY HYPOCRISY

Not so ironic, this is the same Pete Wilson who as California Governor recently vigorously (and successfully) campaigned for the passage of the state's Proposition 187. Unless overturned by the courts, the law will strip illegal aliens of health and welfare benefits and deny schooling to their children.

Reflecting on Wilson's effort, Katie Leishman, writing in the *New York Times,* wonders what might have happened if the election had taken place at a major harvest time when half the state's farm labor force was made up of illegals?

"Farmworkers took part in freedom marches and scattered demonstrations, to no effect; a series of harvest strikes would have been a different matter. Latino leaders often resort to lyrical reminders of how handsomely Mexicans treated those who stole California from them. This kind of cant goes nowhere; but if Cesar Chavez were alive, he would have taken the debate right to the bottom line."

As Wilson's fellow GOP conservative William Bennett notes: "California draws in thousands of migrant (agricultural) workers each year, then complains that some stay. The message is: Come for a few months, then get out. That's not a sensible way to conduct policy."

Yet, as Philip Martin, the University of California agricultural labor scholar, points out, "there's nothing as permanent as a temporary worker." Bernard E. Anderson, the U.S. Department of Labor's Assistant Secretary for Employment Standards, adds, "guest worker programs are often abusive and invariably lead to expanded, not diminished levels of permanent immigration."

Lost in all the political demagoguery surrounding the illegal immigration issue today, however, is the simple fact, as Gustavo De La Vina, chief agent of the U.S. Border Patrol in San Diego points out, "they are coming across to get jobs."

From the fields, to the packing sheds, to the food processing factories of U.S. agribusiness, this seeming lure of jobs for people already living in near destitution in their own economically ravaged country continues to fuel our nation's influx of illegal immigration.

In a country where the currency has lost about half its value against the dollar since the peso was devalued in December 1994, interest rates have soared, bankruptcies have multiplied and over one million people have been forced out of work, as paying jobs have become highly prized.

As the *Wall Street Journal* reports, throughout Mexico – a country where 26% of workers are either unemployed or without full-time jobs – doctors, lawyers, engineers, teachers and other professionals are crossing the border to wait on tables, filling lowly clerical jobs or harvesting American crops.

In that process many of them must brave the New River, near Calexico, California. Across a river covered with white suds, raw sewage from homes in Mexico, industrial waste from U.S.-owned factories in Mexico and chemical poison runoffs from nearby fields, they come. Border Patrol Agent Bleu Siders describes the scene: "It's one of the most polluted rivers in the world. Aliens go in this river; we have to go after them."

CHEAP LABOR

Such cheap workers, no matter what their background, however, have always been welcomed by agribusiness. As Jack Snider, boss of the asparagus packing shed at Black Dog Farms in Holtville, Calif., who has supervised Mexican professionals, such as doctors and lawyers, told the *Wall Street Journal:* "I love professionals. They can diagnose you while you work."

It is no coincidence that more than 70% of legal and illegal immigrants in the U.S. now live in California, Texas, Florida, New York, New Jersey and Illinois, all major agricultural producing states. Likewise, it is also no coincidence that a mere 139,560 farms of the nation's total 1.925 million farms have over 77% of the total U.S. agricultural labor expenses.

It is not just the fields and orchards of the U.S. that draw illegal immigrants, but in recent years there has been a marked increase in their number in the meat and poultry slaughter-houses of the Midwest. In September 1995, 90 such illegals were arrested in a ConAgra beef packing plant in Garden City, Kansas, and in March 125 were arrested at a similar Cargill plant in Schuyler, Nebraska.

Northwestern Arkansas, where such agribusiness giants as Tyson Foods, Hudson Foods, ConAgra and Simmons Industries have major poultry operations, has seen an increase of over 30,000 Hispanic workers just in the past few years attracted by jobs that pay between $6-$7 an hour.

A U.S. government-sponsored Operation South PAW (Protecting American Workers) in September 1995 alone netted some 2,000 illegal aliens across the South. It is estimated by the Immigration and Naturalization Service (INS) that such raids channeled more than $3 million in wages back to U.S. workers.

AGRIBUSINESS

Today, agribusiness both exploits and blames immigrant workers for many of the social ills which pervade our society. But, as John Palacio of the Mexican American Legal Defense and Educational Fund (MALDEF) explains, "Immigrants take jobs Americans don't want. They are not only blamed for economic ills, but exploited for cheap labor. But they contribute much more than they receive."

One 1995 study, sponsored by the Cato Institute, a "libertarian research group," found that each year the average immigrant family adds about $2,500 in taxes to the economy above what it consumes in public costs.

Yet, amidst all the controversy and recent federal and state law making as it applies to immigrants, one important study which gets to the heart of the matter has been all but ignored by the public. In 1992 a bipartisan Commission on Agricultural Workers, created by Congress, set forth six recommendations designed to improve the working conditions for the nation's farm workers.

As their report indicates, it's time that the public understand that the social burden cheap farm labor brings to rural and urban communities should be placed where many economists believe it should be – in the cost of the product itself.

It is time that we acknowledge, as Dan Rather did on CBS-TV's recent documentary "Legacy of Shame," "the brutal human price to be paid for our food," and that we put an end to a system that takes for granted the exploitation of men, women and children for the sake of the so-called "world's cheapest food supply."

Philip Martin, for example, notes in this regard that if the wages of all agricultural workers were doubled, the cost of California produce would rise approximately only 10 percent. This would cost the government nothing, but would increase tax revenues by increasing taxable income at the same time it would lower welfare costs by decreasing the number of families seeking government need-based services.

Also important is the fact that the public needs to recognize that the cheap wages paid to farm laborers and the cheap raw material prices paid to farmers are only enriching the coffers of a select few transnational food manufacturing corporations. Meanwhile, the society as a whole is left to pay an exacting social and economic cost for such exploitation.

AMERICANS WON'T DO THE WORK

James S. Holt

James S. Holt is an economist at the Employment Policy Foundation in Washington, D.C. He serves as a consultant on labor and immigration matters to the National Council of Agricultural Employers. He also spent 16 years on the economics faculty at Penn State University.

■ POINTS TO CONSIDER

1. Discuss the special aspects of agriculture production, according to Holt.

2. How has undocumented labor affected certain agricultural sectors?

3. Does the author believe, under any circumstances, that the United States can fulfill its need for seasonal laborers? Why or why not?

Excerpted from the testimony of James S. Holt before the Subcommittees on Risk Management and Specialty Crops of the House of Representatives Committee on Agriculture and the Subcommittee on Immigration Claims of the House Committee on the Judiciary, December 14, 1995.

As production of labor intensive commodities has expanded, the expansion has been in areas remote from available domestic labor supplies. Seasonal alien migration, including many illegal entrants, met that need.

With rising incomes worldwide, and changes in consumer tastes and preferences favoring fruits and vegetables, the demand for labor intensive agricultural commodities is growing rapidly. United States agricultural producers have participated in that growth. The 1992 United States Census of Agriculture reported that fruits, vegetables and horticultural specialties accounted for more than $23 billion of agricultural sales in 1992, a 32 percent increase from that reported in the previous agricultural census five years earlier. Most economists expect demand for labor intensive agricultural commodities to continue a strong growth pattern.

ALIEN LABOR

Although there is no hard evidence for this, many agricultural economists agree that the availability of labor, especially alien labor illegally entering the United States, has been an important factor facilitating the growth in U.S. labor intensive agricultural production. The U.S. has, in fact, had a *de facto* alien worker program, albeit one that was uncontrolled and unregulated. As production of labor intensive commodities has expanded, the expansion has undoubtedly been in areas of well-suited land resources where the available labor supply had limited expansion and in areas more remote from available domestic labor supplies. Such production could only develop if there was a supply of seasonal labor willing to migrate into the area to perform the seasonal labor intensive tasks. Seasonal alien migration, including many illegal entrants, met that need.

Both the technological constraints and trade barriers to international competition in labor intensive agricultural commodities have fallen away in recent years, and freer trade is clearly a continuing trend. This has increased competition from foreign producers in domestic markets, but has also opened up opportunities for U.S. producers in export markets. An increasing proportion of the expansion in labor intensive agriculture in the United States is for the export market.

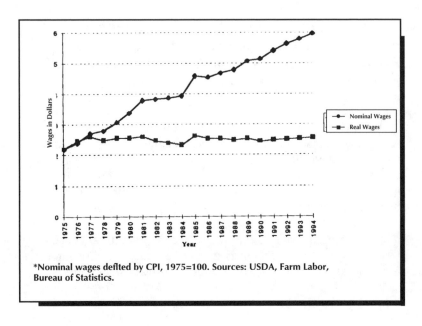

*Nominal wages deflted by CPI, 1975=100. Sources: USDA, Farm Labor,
Bureau of Statistics.

LABOR INTENSIVE

U.S. agricultural production, even most processes in "labor intensive" crops, are highly mechanized. Nevertheless, hired labor costs are a significant proportion of farm production expenses generally. The 1992 Census of Agriculture reported that 690,000 farms hired labor directly and nearly 240,000 incurred contract labor expenses. Hired and contract labor expenses averaged 11.7 percent (one of every eight dollars) of farm production expenses for all U.S. farms.

What makes a commodity "labor intensive" is that its production involves one or more manual-labor-using steps in an otherwise generally mechanized production process. This results in hired labor costs for the commodity being a much larger percentage of total production costs than for other commodities. In the 1992 Census of Agriculture, hired and contract labor costs accounted for 40 percent of total production costs on fruit and nut farms, 37 percent on vegetable farms, and 45 percent on horticultural specialty farms. In some individual commodities the percentage is even higher. Clearly the availability and cost of labor have a major impact on the profitability of these farms and on the production decisions of their operators.

The public policy debate on temporary alien agricultural workers often focuses only on the occupations in which aliens are employed, and overlooks the fact that although some seasonal manual field jobs may be held by aliens, employment in labor intensive agriculture, and employment created by labor intensive agricultural production, extends far beyond these manual field jobs.

DOCUMENTATION

Virtually everyone who is involved in the agricultural labor market or has studied it, has concluded that very little has changed since 1986, and that a significant proportion of the agricultural work force is comprised of illegal aliens working with fraudulent documents. Understandably, this is a difficult phenomenon to research, but some estimates are available.

The U.S. Department of Labor conducts a National Agricultural Worker Survey (NAWS) annually, as a part of which workers are asked to self-identify their legal status. Data synthesized from various NAWS reports show a consistently increasing proportion of unauthorized workers since the survey began. By 1993-94 the percentage was 25 percent.

Data from the NAWS studies indicate that the proportion of undocumented workers has increased by about four to five percentage points annually since 1989. This is roughly consistent with a Commission on Agricultural Workers estimate of "an annual increase of unauthorized worker in the order of approximately six percent." The NAWS estimate of 25 percent undocumented workers in 1993-94 would therefore extrapolate to an estimate of about 30 percent undocumented or fraudulently documented workers in the current U.S. agricultural workforce.

Anecdotal evidence of employer's I-9 forms reported by employers suggests that the self-identified NAWS data is probably the lower limit of the actual percentage of illegal aliens in the agricultural work force. In employer audits INS has identified as many as 50 to 70 percent of documents offered to complete form I-9 as fraudulent. While experience has shown that some of these workers are actually work-authorized, and either the INS's data base is in error or the worker is working under false documents for other reasons than having entered the United States illegally, the proportion of workers who are actually illegal has often exceeded 30 percent. These studies, coupled with field experience, clearly show that an effective system for verifying employment authorization combined with effective enforcement of employer sanctions, will significantly reduce the supply of temporary and seasonal labor for U.S. agriculture.

WAGES

Won't growers be forced to raise wage offers to domestic farmworkers and U.S. residents not now employed to attract additional labor in the absence of aliens? This, of course, is the rationale for many people's opposition to a temporary foreign worker program, and is at the core of the public policy question raised by "guestworker" programs. If the answer to that question were "yes" we would have the best of all possible worlds. Growers could continue in production, more U.S. residents would be employed and farmworker wages would be higher. Unfortunately, however, the answer to the question is "no." Both economic theory and the real world tell us that. Here I will review the practical reasons why the U.S. workforce cannot fill the void.

First it is useful to review the data on farm wage rates. Contrary to common perception, farm work is not minimum wage work. U.S. Department of Agriculture (USDA) reported the U.S. 1994 average hourly earnings for nonsupervisory field workers was $6.02 per hour. For workers paid by piece rate, U.S. average hourly earnings were $7.02 per hour. When they are working, the weekly hours of farmworkers are generally comparable to those of nonfarm workers. For example, in California, where one quarter of all the field workers in the Nation are employed, the 1994 average hourly earnings for nonsupervisory field workers was $6.51 and the average hours of work per week (for those who were working) was 41.5 hours.

U.S. CANNOT FILL THE NEED

Then why don't minimum wage workers abandon their jobs and do farm work at a 40 percent raise? The answer undoubtedly lies in the other characteristics of seasonal farm work. Seasonality itself is foremost among these. While field work pays relatively well on the average when there is work, it is by definition seasonal. Most U.S. workers need and prefer more reliable year round work, and many are obviously willing to take less per hour in order to secure more stability of employment. A second unattractive feature of agricultural work is that many jobs entail physical

MIGRANT NEED

I live in Glennville, Georgia, and have farmed all my life. My brother and I operate a large farming operation in Southeast Georgia. We are involved in produce, tobacco, peanuts, timber and cattle.

My brother and I are true family farmers. I have to take a man or woman's word. If they show me proper documentation, I have to believe them. I do not have the resources to travel to other countries to investigate each and every worker.

Our goal is not to displace U.S. workers by bringing in guest workers. We will hire any local people that are willing and able to do this work. Anyone who has operated a farm or processing facility in Georgia knows that you cannot function without migrant labor. There is not an adequate local labor force to keep our businesses running.

Excerpted from the prepared testimony of Robert Dashner before the Subcommittee on Risk Management and Specialty Crops of the House of Representatives Committee on Agriculture, Dec. 14, 1995.

labor under adverse environmental conditions of heat, cold, sun, rain, etc. It is work that many Americans would be physically incapable of doing on a sustained basis, and that most of the rest would prefer not to do if there are better alternatives available.

Third, and in my view probably the most important factor, is that many seasonal farm jobs are not located within normal commuting distance of most workers. In order to take these jobs workers have to become temporary migrant farm workers. Although there is no data to substantiate this, I believe that this is especially characteristic of the areas where expansion in production of labor intensive commodities has more recently occurred. Not only have we stigmatized migrant farm work in this country, we have spent literally billions of dollars of public money trying to reduce domestic migrancy and "settle out" migrant farm workers. It is not surprising, therefore, that there is a "shortage" of willing U.S. migrant farm workers. Aliens, on the other hand, are willing to migrate, in fact are required to do so to get into the United States.

This should not leave you with the impression that U.S. residents will not do farm work. In fact, the best available data shows that more than two million U.S. residents currently do hired farm work at some time during the year. The problem that we are discussing here is that because of the availability of alien labor, first under circumstances where it was not illegal for employers to employ these aliens, and more recently possessing documents that employers are legally obligated to accept, U.S. agricultural production has expanded beyond the capacity for the U.S. resident work force to meet its needs. That expansion has, of course, been beneficial to the U.S. It has expanded U.S. economic activity and created additional jobs for U.S. residents. But it has left U.S. agriculture dependent on an alien labor supply.

STOLEN YOUTH, DEGRADED CHILDHOOD

Robert Weissman

Robert Weissman is editor of the Multinational Monitor. *The* Multinational Monitor, *founded by Ralph Nader, is a monthly journal that is the watchdog of transnational corporations, global business and trade.*

■ POINTS TO CONSIDER

1. Describe the various types of child labor globally, and the conditions under which it is performed.

2. What is the relationship between poverty, unemployment and child labor, according to the article?

3. Explain the author's contention that globalization proliferates child labor. Discuss this issue in the contexts of both the industrial and agricultural sectors.

4. Discuss the criticism of western nations, in particular, the Structural Adjustment Programs imposed by the World Bank and IMF.

5. What is the author's view on the importation of goods made by children, to the United States?

Robert Weissman, "Stolen Youth: Brutalized Children, Globalization and the Campaign to End Child Labor," **Multinational Monitor**, January/February 1997: 10-6. Reprinted with permission.

Employer desires for cheap and docile labor have existed for centuries. What is new in the child labor equation is economic globalization.

"We cannot possibly gravitate from a condition of agriculturalism to a condition of industrialism without the employment of minors." So testified Lewis Parker, a South Carolina cotton mill owner, before the U.S. House of Representatives Committee on Labor in 1914, in opposition to legislation that would have outlawed the use of child labor in the United States.

THE SCOURGE OF CHILD LABOR

Parker was on the wrong side of history. By the time he testified, most U.S. states had already adopted legislation limiting the use of child labor. In 1916, President Woodrow Wilson signed into law an act regulating the use of child labor in industry. The Supreme Court struck down the law in 1918, but in 1938, with adoption of the Fair Labor Standards Act, the United States banned the use of child labor altogether. While the ban still suffers from serious enforcement problems, the widespread use of child labor in the United States has been effectively eradicated.

Now, six decades later, the child labor debate is being replayed on a global scale – with some Third World business interests and their supporters echoing Parker's arguments – as the world suddenly awakens to the ongoing scourge of child labor.

With economic globalization tying national economies more closely together, awareness of the incidence of child labor in Third World nations is growing rapidly in the industrialized countries, as Northern consumers respond with discomfort to reports showing that the clothes they wear and the toys with which their children play are made by child workers. At the same time, the globalization process which is spurring the new Northern awareness of child labor is putting strains on the economies and social structures of countries in the global South – and, in many ways, intensifying the problem of child labor.

FORCED LABOR AND HAZARDOUS CONDITIONS

Approximately 120 million children under the age of 14 labor full-time, according to a 1996 estimate by the International Labor Organization (ILO), that is widely viewed as the most informed ever. If those for whom work is a secondary activity are included, the number of working children rises to 250 million.

The majority of child laborers live in Asia, although Africa has a higher rate of child labor. The ILO estimates that 40 percent of African children between the ages of five and 14 work. The majority of the 120 million full-time working children labor in the commercial agricultural sector.

Child labor is not confined to any particular economic sector, however. Children work as domestic servants, in mining, as divers in deep-sea fishing, in construction, as prostitutes, in toy, shoe and garment factories, as cigarette makers, as rug weavers, in charcoal making, in glass and ceramic factories, as sports equipment and surgical instrument makers, in the match and fireworks industries and in many other jobs.

The most appalling circumstances of child labor involve forced labor and children working in hazardous conditions. The most common form of forced child labor is debt bondage, a practice by which parents pledge their children's work to pay off debts. The debts are often miniscule, but the children may work for their entire childhood – indeed, for their entire lives – to pay them off because of fraudulent accounting mechanisms employed by debt holders...

SEARCHING FOR CAUSES

It is obvious that poverty and child labor are intertwined. Brutalized child laborers are almost exclusively poor. Children typically work to earn money for their families or to help pay off family debts. And wealthier families do not need or permit their children to labor at the expense of education and physical, intellectual and emotional development. But poverty is not, by itself, the cause of child labor.

The fact that rates of child labor vary dramatically between countries of similar levels of economic development proves this point most clearly. In China, for example, there has been little child labor in recent decades, according to U.S. diplomatic sources. Even though extremely poor until recent years, China made a political decision to put its children in school, rather than on the work rolls. Similarly, Kerala State, in India, the country most famous for abuse of child labor, has virtually abolished child labor...

Many countries have strong traditions of tolerating child labor...

Similarly, discriminatory attitudes toward women and girls may undergird parents' willingness to send their daughters off to prostitution, or to be domestic servants...

GLOBALIZATION AND CHILD LABOR

All of these factors – poverty, cultural traditions, prejudice against ethnic, religious or racial groups, discrimination against girls, inadequate access to education and employer desires for cheap and docile labor – have existed for centuries. What is new in the child labor equation is economic globalization.

The most obvious contribution globalization is making to the increase in child labor is its intensification of price competition for global consumer markets. "This competition makes everyone look for any way they can lower costs," says Oded Grajew, director and president of the Abrinq Foundation for Children's Rights in Brazil. "To have child labor means lower costs; because the wages are very low, children never complain, and they work long hours with no overtime pay."

This unregulated competition is responsible in significant part for children sewing garments in Haiti, Guatemala and Honduras for labels and retailers such as Disney, Kathie Lee Gifford and Wal-Mart and Phillips-Van Heusen, or making toys for sale in the U.S. market – the instances of child labor receiving the greatest attention in the United States in recent years. Even in China, where child labor has long been minimized, there are reports that child labor is increasing rapidly in the low-wage export industries of the Pearl River Delta in the Southeast.

The number of children working in the export-oriented sectors of the economy is small in proportional terms, however. The U.S. Department of Labor pegs it at approximately five percent, although international price competition – including for goods sold domestically in competition with foreign imports and as inputs for products to be exported – may raise the proportion somewhat. There are other, less obvious but still important ways that globalization is contributing to an increase in child labor.

Cheap agricultural exports to the Third World and promotion of export-oriented agriculture in developing countries have rocked the social structure in rural communities across the globe. Relying on violence, coercion or sometimes impersonal market forces, plantation owners have ejected many rural families from their

Among the most hazardous of jobs is scavenging. Children, like this boy in Brazil, collect used paper, plastics, rags and bottles from garbage dumps, selling them to retailers for recycling.

land, depriving them of their livelihood and leaving them with narrow economic options. Some have taken work on plantations, where children are likely to be employed as well; some move to urban slums, where children may search for jobs to support their family; and some send their children to urban areas to earn cash to support the family...

STRUCTURAL ADJUSTMENT

The International Monetary Fund (IMF) and World Bank imposition of structural adjustment policies on Third World economies has strengthened many of the trends contributing to child labor. As a condition for receiving further loans, the IMF and World Bank instruct indebted Third World countries to promote exports and cut government spending.

In many cases, governments pressed by the IMF and World Bank to reduce spending have reduced expenditures for education. In recent years, however, the World Bank in particular has recognized the importance of education and health care, and has urged governments to maintain programs in these areas as "investments in human capital." Now, says Peter Fallon, a World Bank economist currently reviewing the Bank policies relating to child labor, "the Bank tries to protect those sectors insofar as possible."...

The World Bank has also encouraged governments to charge students for attending school, or for books and supplies – a so-called "cost-recovery approach." Even small fees prevent poor families from sending some or all of their children to school, however, and those unable to afford school frequently work. Fallon says the Bank's "cost-recovery approach has been targeted to secondary and post-secondary education, and that you are most concerned about primary education" in seeking to combat child labor.

THE MYTH OF INEVITABILITY

Given the multiple, overlapping causes of child labor, no single approach will end the scourge. Most serious analysts agree that complementary approaches are needed. Yet the belief that child labor is an inevitable consequence of poverty – perhaps necessary to help countries develop economically – and that economic growth is the key to eliminating child labor persists. In June 1996, for example, *USA Today* editorialized that "the West's own history has shown that for backward nations seeking to rise from desperate poverty," it is mechanization and industrialization that solve child labor.

From a rather different vantage point, an international gathering of child laborers meeting in India in November 1996, urged those concerned about child labor to work to alleviate the harsh conditions under which children work, rather than to eliminate child labor altogether.

Pharis Harvey of the International Labor Rights Fund argues that the *USA Today* editorial writers and the child workers at the India meeting have succumbed to the same, mistaken "fatalistic" view of child labor. "Those people believe child labor is the product, rather than a cause, of poverty."

In fact, Harvey argues, "child labor perpetuates poverty, generates it and regenerates it." Children who work become sickly adults, and a drain on national economies. With little if any education, they are less productive workers as adults. And, children fill jobs that adults would otherwise occupy; in every country with high rates of child labor, there is a severe unemployment problem, with adults' skills, creativity and labor power wasted.

Conscious and purposeful intervention is needed to make meaningful inroads in eradicating child labor... Third World national governments have the most important role to play in eliminating child labor. They must enforce national laws banning the use of child labor, provide quality universal education for children and ensure that cultural traditions and prejudices are not allowed to override national commitments to child-free workplaces. The examples of China and Kerala State show what developing countries can do in this area, if they choose.

RICH COUNTRIES AND POOR, WORKING CHILDREN

Most have not chosen to crack down on child labor, but there are increasing possibilities to bring pressure to bear on those who do not act on their own. With national economies becoming more interwoven, the children stitching clothes in Haiti or India or Thailand are more likely than ever before to be doing it for U.S. or German or other industrialized country consumers. That fact gives industrialized country governments and consumers the power to influence Third World country child labor practices.

As Northern consumers have expressed increasing concern about the conditions under which the products they buy are made, many corporations have adopted codes of conduct for their overseas operations and especially for overseas contractors. For its 1996 report, "The Apparel Industry and Codes of Conduct," the U.S. Department of Labor surveyed 42 major garment manufacturers, designers and retailers. It found that 36 had adopted codes of conduct – many or most in recent years – with provisions specifically prohibiting the use of child labor in the manufacture of goods they imported...

A potentially more reliable means of purging goods made with child labor from international commerce are labeling programs. The most prominent child labor-related labeling scheme is the Rugmark program, an international project which certifies carpets are made without use of child labor. Independent inspectors validate that carpet looms do not use child labor; certified carpets bear the Rugmark smiley face logo; and a slight additional charge for Rugmark-approved carpets goes to fund not only inspections but programs to put children who might otherwise be weaving rugs into schools...

Not all internationally traded goods lend themselves to labeling, however, and despite Rugmark's considerable success, the delays in getting the program off the ground and the voluntary nature of the program suggest the labeling approach will not be a comprehensive solution to child labor, even in international markets.

A different, more direct approach does hold out the possibility of a comprehensive solution: a flat-out ban on the importation of goods made with child labor. In the last several sessions of the U.S. Congress, Harkin and Brown have introduced the Child Labor Deterrence Act (commonly known as the Harkin Bill), which would enact such a ban in the United States, and funnel $10 million to ILO programs to eliminate child labor.

"Without the passage of the Child Labor Deterrence Act," says Darlene Adkins, coordinator of the Washington, D.C.-based Child Labor Coalition, "the best we can expect is a piecemeal approach to curtailing the import of items made by exploited children, and consumers who want child labor-free products will remain frustrated in the marketplace."

CHALLENGING CHILD LABOR

U.S. adoption of the Harkin Bill approach would go a long way toward eliminating child labor from the production of goods intended to enter into international trade. But child laborers in export-oriented production make up only a small portion of child laborers. A comprehensive approach to abolishing child labor will require not only intervention by industrialized country consumers and governments, but strong political commitments by Third World governments. Whether they can muster that political commitment in an era when the pressures of globalization are exacerbating the conditions leading to the use of child labor remains to be seen.

BLANKET CONDEMNATION HELPS NO ONE

Chris Brazier

Chris Brazier edited the July 1997 issue of the New Internationalist *(NI), and he spent part of 1996 editing the State of the World's Children report for UNICEF. NI is a monthly international journal which reports on poverty, inequality and the relationship between rich and poor nations.*

■ POINTS TO CONSIDER

1. Discuss some of the misconceptions about the term "child labor," according to Brazier.

2. Are their distinctions between the labor of children in the North v. South?

3. Explain the author's view concerning boycotts. Compare and contrast this view with that of the previous reading.

4. The author suggests possible ideas to curtail the most dangerous forms of child labor. Identify these and evaluate.

Excerpted from Chris Brazier, "Respite – and Respect," **The New Internationalist**, July 1997, pp. 7-10. Reprinted by permission, **New Internationalist,** Toronto. Subscription (Canada) $38.50 (includes $2.94 GST) – individual 1 year, $64.20 (includes $4.20 GST) institution 1 year – $60.00, 35 Riviera Drive, Unit 17, Markham, ON L3R 8N4, (905) 946-0407, (905) 946-0410 (fax), magazine @ indas.on.can. Subscription (United States) $35.98 – individual 1 year, $60.00 – institution 1 year, PO Box 1143, Lewiston, NY 14092, (905) 946-0407, (905) 946-0410 (fax).

If we treat all work by children as equally unacceptable, we are trivializing the issue and making it less likely that we will be able to root out the most damaging forms of child labor.

"Child labor." I wonder what image those two words conjure up in your mind. My guess is that it will bring forth two images in parallel. On the one hand the children of Victorian Britain locked in their dark satanic mills as the Industrial Revolution took hold. On the other, children from India or Pakistan today, also chained to looms and forced to endure harrowing conditions. And against these nightmarish images are probably counterposed the children of Western societies, freed from the necessity of work, enjoying free education and free play.

Yet if we are not careful these potent images will lead us into a blind alley – one marked "complacency." People in the rich world tend to assume that child labor, like slavery, is something that was abolished in the rich world about a century ago and that it only exists now in developing countries – and this certainty leads them to feel they can preach from the moral high ground to poorer countries still locked in their medieval castles of ignorance and backwardness...

The standard view would be that while this kind of harmless work for pocket money certainly takes place, there is no dangerous "child labor" in the North. The same view would be likely to maintain that work done by children in the South is more often than not hazardous and exploitative. Actually both these statements are untrue – and examining why will show that "child labor" is an altogether more complex and less clear-cut issue than is normally supposed.

North...Examples of hazardous child labor can unfortunately still be found in most rich countries – and their incidence is probably increasing rather than decreasing. The reason this kind of child work is largely removed from public notice – or that a blind eye is turned towards it – is that it takes place largely within ethnic-minority or immigrant groups. In the US, for example, immigrant children, usually of Hispanic origin, routinely take part in agricultural work, especially at harvest time; in Britain they are more likely to be South Asian children doing piece-work at home or in garment sweatshops; in Greece they are likely to be of gypsy or Albanian origin.

A schoolroom in Burkina Faso.

There is one highly damaging variety of work, though, which is extremely visible and is rife in all rich countries: child prostitution. It is illegal but the laws tend not to be enforced and the economic and social conditions that produce it go unchallenged. And somehow nobody ever conceives of it as a form of child labor...

...and South: Most of the world's hazardous and exploitative child labor, it is true, takes place in the South. At its most extreme it is a modern form of slavery, from the children forced to labor on the sugarcane estates of northeast Brazil to those the Burmese military government has ordered to work on a new railroad. In the Indian subcontinent this virtual slavery is institutionalized in the shape of "bonded" child labor, which sees children as young as eight or nine pledged by their parents to employers in payment of a debt.

One of the most notorious examples of bonded child labor is the carpet industry of the Indian state of Uttar Pradesh where, according to a recent study, thousands of children in the carpet industry are "kept in captivity, tortured and made to work for 20 hours a day without a break. Little children are made to crouch on their toes, from dawn to dusk every day, severely stunting their growth during formative years. Social activists in the area find it hard to work because of the strong mafia-like control that the car-pet loom owners have on the area."

The continued existence of working conditions like these is a deep stain on human civilization – and any action to eliminate child labor has to concentrate first and foremost on cases like these. Yet it is vital to recognize that the majority of work done by children in the Third World is neither so hazardous nor so exploitative. This is why the term "child labor" is too explosive and negative to be applied to all work by children...

CHILDREN'S CONTRIBUTION

Indeed, some kinds of child work are useful, positive contribu-tions to child development. The idea that childhood should be an entirely work-free zone is a luxurious and rather sentimental Western idea. Work for a few hours a day that contributes to the family's well-being – whether by performing domestic duties or helping in the family fields – is more likely to foster a child's development than to damage it.

And between the two extremes of positive and negative child work – in a grey area less susceptible to cut-and-dried judgment as to whether it is exploitative or damaging – come the vast majority of children's occupations in all their multiplicity and diversity. Children haul water and collect firewood. They deliver newspapers and tea. They take care of younger siblings. They work on the streets washing windshields, shining shoes or selling cigarettes. They can be found in sweatshops or in their family's sewing room. They are servants in the homes of the better-off.

If we treat all work by children as equally unacceptable, we are trivializing the issue and making it less likely that we will be able to root out the most damaging forms of child labor: blanket con-demnation helps no one. People in the rich world consider work by their own children to be acceptable when it is performed for pocket money to buy computer games. It would be thoroughly bizarre if Westerners who allowed their own children to work for pocket money to buy compact discs should seek to outlaw child work in the Third World which is often driven by a poor family's desperate need. In every country, rich or poor, it is the nature and conditions of children's work which determines whether or not they are exploited – not the plain fact of their working...

A CHILD'S STORY

Delwar is 12 years old. Pressed by overseas groups to stop employing children, Delwar's factory in the Bangladeshi capital fired him last September, along with his young co-workers. But it didn't do Delwar much good. He now ekes out a living selling waste paper that he picks up along the roadside.

Delwar and his mother, a mentally ill beggar, sorely miss his $20-a-month factory salary. They live with his half-brother's family, eight people jammed into a one-room, dirt-floored hovel. Lately they have been skipping meals. For two months, they haven't been able to pay the rent...

But Delwar's story is a cautionary tale for those fighting to help Asia's youngest workers. Child labor is a complex problem, and simple, well-meaning solutions can sometimes do more harm than good.

Gordon Fairclough, "It Isn't Black and White," **Far Eastern Economic Review**, March 7, 1996: 54-7.

VIABLE SOLUTIONS?

So what action should we take to combat child labor? The current media furor in the West about child labor makes people want to leap into action. And the most natural weapons to reach for are understandably boycotts or trade sanctions – these are often, after all, tactics which this magazine would favor, in response, for example, to gross human rights abuses.

But, like aid programs, anti-child labor initiatives must adapt to local conditions. All attempts to cure Third World problems are doomed to do more harm than good if they are designed in the air-conditioned offices of Western capitals. The battle against child labor is no exception.

Who would oppose, for example, the notion that employers in Bangladesh's garment industry should be barred from using children's labor? Surely we're on safe ground here – this is hardly the stuff of which heavy-handed development disasters are made. Wrong: when children (most of them girls) were expelled from the garment factories as a result of US pressure in 1993, their families' poverty drove them to more desperate avenues of employment – on the streets, in smaller, more hazardous workshops, or even, some claim, to prostitution…the implications of which have fundamentally altered the approach to child labor of the key UN agencies.

It is clear that any program of eliminating child labor which does not provide reasonable alternatives for the child workers it ousts – which simply casts them out of a workplace they had only entered due to extreme poverty – is dumping on them from the moral high ground an avalanche of negative consequences.

EDUCATION OPTIONS

But the goal clearly has to be to stop children entering exploitative work in the first place, which is why education is bound to be the key to any serious programs against child labor. We need an education system in the developing world as different from the current one as the sun is from the moon – one that is properly resourced and valued, that reaches the poorest children, not just in terms of geography but in terms of hearts and minds, that expands their horizons beyond the gate marked "drudgery."

The world needs to recover its passion for providing decent, relevant education for all children – instead of accepting that educational provision will suffer death by a thousand public spending cuts in the rich world as well as the poor...

Education of this empowering kind can help prevent a child from being trapped by an exploitative employer – and, after all, it is exploitation rather than poverty alone which generates child labor. If there were no employers prepared to exploit children, there would be no child labor. Children are more easily intimidated, less likely to organize in trade unions – and can be paid much less. This allows employers to put their products on the market at the cheapest possible prices – thereby undercutting any company which offers decent wages and conditions to adults. In an increasingly globalized economy, the scramble for competitiveness is even more crazed, which is one reason why pious condemnations of child labor by enthusiasts for free trade and globalization in Washington seldom play to great applause in the Majority World.

READING

11

SWEATSHOPS FOR THE WORLD'S POOR

Joyce Bowers

Joyce Bowers is on the Board of Directors for the Resource Center of the Americas and facilitates a workshop at the Center on Child Labor in Minneapolis. The Resource Center of the Americas is a nonprofit organization dedicated to education and action in the Americas, 317 Seventeenth Avenue SE, Minneapolis, MN, 55414-2077, (612) 627-9445, (612) 627-9450 (fax) and rctamn@tc.umn.edu, www.americas.org/rctal.

■ POINTS TO CONSIDER

1. Analyze Bowers' response to critics of child labor opponents.

2. Discuss the role low-wage and child laborers play in the global economy.

3. According to the author, explain the effects Structural Adjustment Programs have on nations of the global south.

4. Compare and contrast crusades of the Nineteenth Century with those of today.

Joyce Bowers, "The Cruelest Myth," **Connection to the Americas**, May 1997: 1-2. **Connection to the Americas** is a publication of the Resource Center of the Americas, Minneapolis, Minnesota. Reprinted by permission of the Resource Center of the Americas.

***Our job in the First World is to recognize the systems
behind child labor and devise strategies to attack the
problem at its roots.***

The tiny, barefoot girl turns her head toward the camera, but her
deft fingers continue automatically adjusting the threads of the
spinning jenny. Her face is absolutely blank. Toiling in a Lowell,
Massachusetts, textile mill, she is one of thousands of U.S. child
workers photographed by Lewis Hine early this century.

DEJA VU

Hine did his job so well that I can imagine his subject looking
straight through me into the other photograph I hold, into the eyes
of a Pakistani girl, also barefoot, squatting before a carpet loom. The
Pakistani has raised vacant eyes to the camera, but her hands still
fly among the carpet's bright threads. This photo was taken in 1995.

Both girls are from their countries' lowest classes. They are
probably illiterate and will never grow to their full stature, even if
they survive the respiratory diseases they've likely contracted. Yet
both might tell us that, as much as they hate their looms, they're
lucky to have work. Their families desperately need the money.

The photos, then, seem to support a common refrain of free-
marketers. No one is happy that children are working under gruel-
ing conditions, they say, but poverty demands it. Work is better
than starvation. All rich countries went through this disturbing-
but-necessary phase of industrial development and owe their
present wealth to it. What's more, say many conservative Third
World economists, well-off consumers in developed nations have
no business trying to "free the children," especially given the
devastation already wrought in the southern hemisphere by U.S.
and European governments.

In this vein, Guatemalan economist Lucy Martínez-Mont
suggested in the *Wall Street Journal* that banning imports of child-
made goods would eliminate jobs, hike labor costs, drive plants
from poor countries and increase debt. Rich Northerners, she said,
would soothe their consciences by sabotaging Third World industrialization and denying poor children any hope of a better future.

So, when the eyes of that little Pakistani carpet weaver make us
want to march to Dayton's and set fire to every rug in the place,
are we short-sighted, even selfish? I don't think so, any more than

85

I think U.S. children's rights campaigners of the early-20th century were misguided. Responding to suffering is never out of line. But to stem child labor at its roots, clearly we must unravel the "necessary phase of development" argument.

STARTING POINT

Shackles: The obvious starting point is understanding that today's child workers are players in a global economy. They live in nations that have little ability to set their own economic and social policies. Their governments, shackled by trade agreements and debt, are forced to take orders from international lending institutions.

In general, capital comes and goes freely, country to country, always seeking lower costs and greater profits. It often flows toward poorer nations that carry a large debt, nations invariably saddled by World Bank loan conditions and an International Monetary Fund Structural Adjustment Program. The agencies, both dominated by the United States, force debtor nations to increase exports and decrease social spending.

Although the U.S. Labor Department estimates that only about five percent of child workers are directly involved in export industries, Structural Adjustment exacerbates child labor in the rest of the economy. For example, the land concentration necessary for export agriculture drives out poor families that had survived through subsistence farming. Left with no means of support, they move to cities in search of work, dramatically expanding the pool of unemployed.

Children, who can be paid less, are more likely to be hired than a family's adult members. Far from employing all available hands, most of today's developing countries couple child labor with high adult unemployment. One problem feeds off the other, to the enormous profit of employers.

BANK LENDING AND STRUCTURAL ADJUSTMENT

Although World Bank lending policies don't officially encourage child labor, the bank's rigid cost-control requirements make hiring children advantageous. Loans often go to economic sectors, such as Mexican handicrafts, that are rife with child workers. The World Bank has even encouraged governments to charge a fee for public education, which forces many struggling families to send children into the workforce instead of to school.

UNICEF/5530/Isaac

The long hours and strains of carpet weaving cause muscular disease and deformities, and the inhalation of carpet fiber and chemicals leads to respiratory infections. A boy in Afghanistan works at a loom.

If a government enforces child labor laws or demands family-supporting wages, it faces capital flight from the country. Transnational companies move their plants to hire workers at just a few cents per hour less. If a debtor country resists structural adjustment, the International Money Fund (IMF) or World Bank may halt funding. The history of U.S. intervention in Latin America, moreover, shows that disobedient countries may face even worse punishment.

Billionaires: Early in the century, when a combative U.S. movement finally mounted pressure to outlaw child labor, establish compulsory education and set an adult minimum wage, federal and state governments were able to comply. Back then, no international agency applied pressure to stop enforcement. Companies were also limited in their ability to pack up and leave the country.

Even so, pools of cheap labor were maintained, largely by enforcing racial, ethnic, gender and geographical divisions among workers. Today's transnational capital would easily maintain its cheap labor pool in the Third World.

It's true that widespread U.S. child labor preceded tremendous development and wealth in the country. But the affluence has never been shared among all, and has actually concentrated into ever fewer hands. While more than one in five U.S. kids now grows up

SERVING THE GLOBAL ECONOMY

Some children work with toxic glues to assemble shoes, toil in hellish glass factories, weave silk threads, pour molten brass into molds, or clean the poisonous barrels of leather-tanning fluids. Hundreds of thousands labor in brickyards, quarries and mines, bearing burdens far too heavy for their slender bodies, contracting silicosis, tuberculosis and other diseases. The International Labor Organization (ILO) estimates that around 200 million children are engaged in work that is dangerous to their health, morals or development.

Pharis J. Harvey, "Where Children Work: Child Servitude in the Global Economy," **Christian Century**, April 5, 1995.

---

poor, CEOs make 212 times the average U.S. worker's wage, up from 44 times in 1965. Last year, former Disney CEO Michael Eisner clocked in at $97,600 an hour, and Mattel CEO John Amerman at $1,801. The nation's average worker earned less than $12, and the minimum wage employee made only $4.75.

A related myth is that U.S. industrialization ended child exploitation. Some one million kids, mostly the children of migrant farm workers, are laboring in U.S. fields today, according to the United Farm Workers of America. They attend school sporadically, if at all. Other kids toil in the garment industry, working for a piece rate in urban sweatshops or at home. These are children mainly of immigrants who themselves have come here for economic opportunity.

When a nation's elite claims the country will benefit from something, it's fair to ask just who they mean. Since the North American Free Trade Agreement (NAFTA) took effect in 1994, Mexico has become the world's fifth wealthiest nation if measured by the number of billionaires. But the number of children working in Mexico City has increased 100 percent.

Many of the strongest advocates for the world's working children, and for consumer pressure on their behalf, are themselves from the Third World. To these organizers, child labor is not a necessary step out of poverty, but a means of perpetuating it. Our job in the First World is to recognize the systems behind child labor and devise strategies to attack the problem at its roots.

OPPORTUNITY SHOPS FOR THE DISPOSSESSED

Hans F. Sennholz

Hans F. Sennholz wrote the following article for The Freeman, *a publication of the Foundation for Economic Education, Inc. (FEE). The Foundation is an organization advocating private property, the free market, and limited government, Irvington-on-Hudson, New York, 10533, (914) 591-7230, (914) 591-8910 (fax), freeman@westnet.com, www.fee.org.*

■ **POINTS TO CONSIDER**

1. Explain the author's view of the development of the modern American economy.

2. Discuss the "unintended consequences" of labor advocates' activities.

3. Explain the issue of "protectionism."

4. Contrast the "old" and "new" world orders as the author views them.

Hans F. Sennholz, "Sweatshops for the New World Order," **The Freeman**, November 1996, Notes from FEE. © 1996 The Foundation for Economic Education, Inc.

...what Americans call "slave wages," foreign workers may welcome as "living wages."

Poverty is an anomaly to many Americans. When they encounter it in foreign countries, they view it as an aberration of human relations: the rich are exploiting the poor who are forced to work for "slave labor." In contemporary terminology, "profit-seeking multinational corporations are operating monstrous sweatshops for the New World Order."

What these Americans call "sweatshops," the workers in those workplaces may actually hail as "opportunity shops"; and what Americans call "slave wages," foreign workers may welcome as "living wages." The descriptions seem to vary according to the height from which the earnings are viewed. Americans whose wage rates and standards of living are among the highest in the world, always look down on the lower earnings of other nationals. Their lofty perspective invites hasty and disparaging explanations. Looking down on poor and primitive workshops they see "sweatshops" paying "slave wages."

RISING LIVING STANDARDS

A little historical knowledge would help these critics to come down from their lofty perches. During the last century and earlier, our forefathers labored long hours in shabby factories and dangerous mines with primitive tools and equipment, earning wages even lower than those paid in poor countries today. It took many decades of economic development to arrive at current levels of productivity and income. It took several generations of Americans to save and accumulate the productive capital that built our modern apparatus of production. The savings of the people and the business profits that were reinvested by capitalists together with the technological improvements by inventors built the economy as we know it today.

Politicians who always labor for the next election are quick to take credit for the improvements. The phenomenal rise in American wage rates and working conditions, they claim, was the sweet fruit of their own efforts, their labor legislation and regulation. Wise and courageous politicians, they want us to believe, fought valiantly for higher wages and better working conditions. The chorus of these politicians is often sounded out by the agents of labor unions who are singing the praises of their efforts in the

In Thailand, a boy sews garments

form of collective bargaining, violent strikes, and costly boycotts. Both groups often cooperate and give credit to each other for pointing the way and forcing greedy employers to pay American wage rates.

CRITICS' AGENDA

The main activity of politicians and labor leaders is criticizing their opponents. If they actually could improve the working conditions of all workers, they could eradicate the hunger and want of this world, purge all poverty, and bring prosperity to everyone. American legislators and union organizers could bring American working conditions to every corner of the world, from Burundi to Bangladesh.

In reality, working conditions and wage rates depend on labor productivity, which is a direct function of the stock of capital invested per worker. Unless they themselves made investments in their equipment, American workers made no contribution whatsoever to their high standards of living. Wherever they opposed the introduction of modern equipment, or their union agents and political representatives fought or taxed it, they actually resisted the rise in productivity and improvements in their own working conditions.

It was rising labor productivity that liberated women and children from the early sweatshops. In the industrial countries, labor legislation merely sanctioned the improvements brought about by capital investments. Naturally, legislators, regulators, and union officials claimed credit for the changes.

Their loud denunciation of child labor in poor countries usually produces unintended consequences. It may actually hurt the very people it is intended to help. The children who are dismissed or never hired usually do not return to school. On the contrary, they are likely to seek new employment in the underground economy that pays lower wages and makes more physical demands than the "sweatshops." Many children manage to return to the shops by buying fake documents that make them older than they actually are.

UNDERLYING MOTIVATIONS

Few American critics of "monstrous sweatshops" are motivated by their concern for foreign children. They rarely offer to house, clothe, and educate the children after they have been driven out, or merely inquire into the fate of those who have been given the gate. This glaring lack of concern clearly indicates that many critics of foreign child labor are more interested in protecting jobs in the United States than in improving the lot of foreign children. They are old-fashioned "protectionists" who seek to disguise their odious intentions in the sweet talk of great love for children.

Their protectionist agenda also is visible in their open hostility toward "the new world order." No matter what we may think of the new order, it is preferable by far to the "old order" of war or preparation for war. The cataclysmic polarization between the democratic and dictatorial worlds, which generated two world wars and numerous lesser wars, has given way to the worldwide dominion of democracy under the leadership of one world power, the United States. The new order created a world of unprecedented interconnection and economic interaction. National trade barriers have come down significantly, which has led to a great extension of international cooperation and division of labor. The new information technology has brought the light of individual enterprise and the market order to all countries, and a new transportation technology has drawn them closer together than ever before.

ERRONEOUS PERCEPTIONS

With wages that start at less than 40 cents an hour, the apparel plants here offer little by American standards. But many of the people who work in them, having come from jobs that pay even less and offer no benefits or security, see employment here as the surest road to a better life...

What residents of a rich country like the United States see as exploitation can seem a rare opportunity to residents of a poor country like Honduras, where the per capita income is $600 a year and unemployment is 40 percent. Such conflicts of standards and perceptions have become increasingly common as the global economy grows more intertwined, and have set off a heated debate about international norms of conduct and responsibility.

Larry Rohter, "Hondurans in 'Sweatshops' See Opportunity," **New York Times**, Late Ed., July 18, 1996.

SYMBIOTIC RELATIONSHIP

Many millions of people in the developing countries now are laboring diligently and joyfully for Americans. Foreign and American capitalists have built thousands of assembly plants giving employment to people who heretofore had depended on charity or had toiled for mere survival. In exchange for their efforts, several million American workers have found employment in efficient American export industries. Both parties to the exchange, Americans as well as foreigners, benefit visibly from the trade. In fact, the new world order with its great improvements in the international division of labor has helped to offset the horrendous burdens placed on the American economy by the New Deal, Fair Deal, New Republicanism, New Frontier, and all other new political calamities. If it had not been for the phenomenal expansion of world trade with its new "sweatshops," many of us would be unemployed and all of us immeasurably poorer.

READING

13

RETAILERS' RACE TO THE BOTTOM

Charles Kernaghan

Charles Kernaghan is Executive Director of the National Labor Committee.

■ POINTS TO CONSIDER

1. Discuss the abuses of labor mentioned in the article.

2. What is the connection between the retailers and the maquiladores, according to Kernaghan?

3. Define the most important conditions to which factories and retailers must submit.

Excerpted from the testimony of Charles Kernaghan, before the Subcommittee on International Operations and Human Rights of the House of Representatives Committee on International Relations, June 11, 1996.

There is a problem with the fact that the retailers and multi-nationals search the world for misery.

Just to put some of this into perspective, I think it is important to note that approximately one-half of all the apparel purchased in the United States last year, over $190,000,000,000 worth of apparel, was comprised of imports made offshore.

In Central America and the Caribbean alone, there are 500,000 workers, mostly young women, producing apparel exclusively for sale in the United States. Honduras has a population of about two percent of the United States. It exports to the United States twice as much apparel as the United States exports to four countries in Europe – Italy, Germany, the United Kingdom and France combined.

FREE TRADE ZONES

Honduras has 65,000 to 70,000 *maquiladora* workers or assembly workers. We estimate that about 13 percent of those workers are between 12 and 15 years of age. In fact, if you go to the free trade zones in Honduras or to the factories, you will see used school buses from the United States transporting the workers to work.

If you are out in front of the zones in the morning and you see the used school buses from the United States pull up with the English writing still on them and out come hundreds of kids, you think you are at a junior high school. You are not. You are at factories where workers are going in frequently to work 12- to 14-hour shifts producing goods for export to the United States.

You may have heard about the Global Fashion plant and some of the conditions in that factory. Of course, they were making this Kathie Lee garment. Not only was it Kathie Lee. They were also making this jacket by Eddie Bauer, which Eddie Bauer said they were not making in Honduras. But I understand recently they have admitted they are producing there.

GLOBAL SCOPE

It is not just Global Fashion. You can go down the road to a place called Selin Baracoa where minors 14 and 15 years old are employed in that factory, another Korean-owned maquiladora, producing clothing on the Jaclyn Smith line for Kmart. It is the same situation, frequently working from 7 in the morning until 9 at night. There are always armed guards at these factories. Workers are prohibited from going to night school if they must work the overtime.

Other factories I could mention would be Paulsen Garments where this McKids shirt was made. This factory has frequently hired children. The Orion plant in the Galaxy Industrial Park had a lot of minors working in it. They made this Gitano shirt. In fact, I was there in 1995 when the workers went in at 7:30 on Saturday morning and worked 23 hours straight, coming out at 6 on Sunday morning.

It is not by any means just Honduras, and there is no reason to target any country singly like that. Of course, there are minors in El Salvador working. There are minors in Guatemala working. There are children working in Bangladesh and India and Pakistan.

In fact, in Guatemala a *Wall Street Journal* correspondent was there and came upon a plant called Sam Lucas where clothing was being made for Wal-Mart for children. In El Salvador, in a place called Gabo in the San Marcos free trade zone, children's clothing was being made by minors. This is a school code label by Dayton-Hudson. Fourteen-and 15-year-olds were making children's clothing. They also were making a Pebble Beach shirt, which is a Marshalls label. It is a problem that goes well beyond Kathie Lee Gifford.

Of course, in the plant right next door called Mandarin, we found Eddie Bauer again. T-shirts were being made by 14-and 15-year-olds who were sometimes working straight from 7 in the morning until 4 the next day and then sleeping on the ground next to their sewing machines.

INDEPENDENT MONITORING

This plant also produced for J.C. Penney and for The Gap until The Gap laid down the law with Mandarin and brought in independent human rights monitors. The Gap became the first company we know of anywhere in the world which has said to its contractor, "we have nothing to fear." They said we want to respect workers' rights. We do not want children working. We do not want to violate human rights. They opened the factory to independent human rights observers and monitors. I think the U.S. people are not interested in purchasing products made by children, by

At a large refuse dump in Cambodia, a girl collects waste she can sell for recycling.

exploited women, by people paid starvation wages, by people working in illegal sweatshops. This has been proven over and over again.

Recently, we had the opportunity to meet with Mrs. Gifford and her lawyers and her public relation handlers. It was very interesting because Mrs. Gifford asked Wendy Diaz, a 15-year-old Honduran working at Global Fashions, to tell her story. Wendy told Mrs. Gifford the story of what it was like to work in that factory.

By the time Wendy had finished, Mrs. Gifford apologized to Wendy and said to Wendy, "I want you to understand I did not know this was happening. I did not know what was going on." She said, "I am sorry, and I want to give you my word that this will never happen again. I want to work with you, and I want to work with other people that you work with to clean up these factories. If I cannot, I am getting out of the industry."

This is what she told us, and then she went on to Wal-Mart and said, "I want you to return to Honduras. I want my clothing line back in that factory, but I want that factory cleaned up, and I want independent human rights monitors to have access to the factory. I want to pay the workers a living wage."

NOTHING TO HIDE

We are waiting on Wal-Mart now to see what happens, but surely if companies wanted to end sweatshop conditions or child labor, they could immediately open their factories to independent monitors. If they have nothing to be afraid of, then independent human rights organizations on the ground in those countries should have access to the plants.

Of course, all the other excellent things that were said about the "No Sweat" label would be a real breakthrough. We could finally purchase clothing and products that we knew were not made by children or not made by exploited women or made in sweatshops. And we should all support Congressman Moran's law to make countries implement their child labor laws if they are to continue to receive U.S. funding.

There is, of course, a much bigger problem. The large retailers and multi-nationals actually search the world looking for misery. They will tell you themselves that where there is the greatest unemployment, you are always going to find the lowest wages.

The Wal-Marts and the Kmarts and Nikes and the mass industries, trot the world looking for the lowest wages, whether that is in Honduras at 31 cents an hour, Nicaragua at 24 cents an hour, El Salvador at 56 cents an hour, Sri Lanka at 18 cents an hour, or China at 11 cents. They have these Third World countries competing against each other. Who will accept the lowest wages? Who will have the lowest wages and the most miserable working conditions? The multi-nationals that go into Honduras do not even pay taxes. Wal-Mart, a $97,000,000,000 retailer, produces clothing in Honduras without paying one single cent in taxes.

RETURNING TO THE U.S.

It is a system that now is coming back to the United States again. Everybody is beginning to recognize it. The growth of the sweatshops offshore comes back to the United States. We see it in New York and Los Angeles and Boston. We see the retailers telling U.S. manufacturers that they have to meet the same prices that they are paying offshore in these Third World countries. This is one of the reasons we lost 99,000 apparel jobs last year.

I think that Mrs. Gifford's statement, for example, about the independent monitoring was very brave. She has taken on one of

WORKING FOR KATHIE LEE

My name is Wendy Diaz. I'm 15 years old. I was born January 24, 1981. I'm from Honduras. I started working at Global Fashion when I was 13 years old.

Last year, up to December, I worked on Kathie Lee pants. At Global Fashion there are about 100 minors like me – 13, 14, 15 years old – some even 12. On the Kathie Lee pants we were forced to work, almost every day, from 8 a.m. to 9 p.m. On Saturday we worked to 5 p.m. Sometimes they kept us all night long working, until 6:30 a.m. This happened a lot with the Kathie Lee pants. For the girls in the packing department, working these hours was almost constant. Working all these hours I made at most 240 lempiras a week, which I am told is about $21.86 U.S. My base wage is 3.34 lempiras – which is 31 U.S. cents. No one can survive on these wages.

The treatment at Global Fashion is very bad. The supervisors scream at us and yell at us to work faster. Sometimes they throw the garment in your face, or grab and shove you. They make you work very fast, and if you make the production quota one day then they just increase it the next day.

Excerpted from the testimony of Wendy Diaz before the Subcommittee on International Operations and Human Rights of the House of Representatives Committee on International Relations, June 11, 1996.

the biggest retailers in the world. It will be very interesting to see what Wal-Mart and other companies do. Walt Disney pays workers in Haiti who make Walt Disney garments 28 cents an hour, which is truly a starvation wage. It is not said lightly. You cannot live in Haiti on 28 cents an hour. We are asking Walt Disney to work with its contractors to pay 58 cents an hour. This is what the workers are asking for. It is not such a tremendous jump.

NO NEED FOR CHILDREN

If retailers and manufacturers begin to pay a living wage in these countries, sweatshops would be a thing of the past, and so would child labor because they could hire their parents. They do not need these 14-year-olds working in Honduras. If they paid a living wage, they could hire their parents, and the kids could go back to school where they belong. It is nonsense to think that companies have to hire children.

LABOR RIGHTS

I have an internal report here from the United States Agency for International Development (USAID), 1993. To quote, "In Honduras where the maquiladora plants work in industrial plant settings, guards in the private sector parks routinely prohibit entry to union organizers and even to labor inspectors. In both Honduras and Guatemala, it is widely believed in reported labor circles that attempts to organize unions in non-union plants will result in dismissal if discovered."

The report goes on. "In any event, with high rates of unemployment, labor inspection all but absent and without unions to protest in-plant infractions, other worker rights dealing with maximum hours, health, safety, women and child labor, have little or no chance of effective enforcement." The report goes on to say that Honduras has 99 labor inspectors for the entire country. They are most often barred from entering the industrial parks in which the maquiladoras operate.

Slave Labor, Child Labor, and the Maquiladores

RETAILERS' OPPOSITION TO EXPLOITATION

Robert Hall and Kathie Lee Gifford

Robert Hall is the Vice President and International Trade Counsel of the National Retail Federation (NRF). NRF is the world's largest retail trade association, representing all fifty state retail associations and 34 national retail associations. Kathie Lee Gifford is a television entertainer. The line of women's apparel bearing her name came under fire for being produced by Central American sweatshop labor.

■ POINTS TO CONSIDER

1. Why does Hall refer to labeling campaigns as "band-aid" remedies?

2. Explain why working conditions are important to retailers, according to Hall. Why is he critical of the author of the previous reading?

3. Discuss the appropriate chain of action for addressing labor concerns, as outlined in the article. Identify the benefits and loopholes of this chain.

4. How does Kathie Lee Gifford explain the problem of sweatshops? What was her role?

5. Outline Gifford's plan to watch abuses at production sites.

Excerpted from the testimony of Robert Hall and Kathie Lee Gifford before the Subcommittee on International Operations and Human Rights of the House of Representatives Committee on International Relations, June 11 and 15, 1996.

I am an entertainer who had a simple idea...create fashion wear with my name on it to help raise money for charity. In hindsight I would conclude that an explanation of quantum physics is far simpler.

TESTIMONY OF ROBERT HALL

I testify on a matter of extreme importance to American families and the retailers who serve them – the perception of the prevalence of apparel sweat shops generally and those that use child labor specifically.

The nation's retailers abhor the use of child labor, forced labor or exploitative labor wherever it may occur – here in the United States or internationally. Yet, I encourage you and your panel to proceed with caution as you contemplate what types of action that Congress or the Administration can take to curb the abuses that have been outlined by Mr. Kernaghan of the National Labor Committee and Ms. Diaz, (an Honduran teenaged factory worker). A "quick-fix" remedy or band-aid, such as a labeling program, may make American consumers feel good about their purchases – yet, recent history has shown that labeling programs do little to help the plight of those in need of protection – the workers themselves.

REPUTATION AND CONSUMER TRUST

The retail industry goes to extraordinary lengths working with suppliers and contractors, to ensure that the products on our shelves are produced in accordance with all applicable laws. This is not something we take lightly. As retailers, we rely on our reputations and the good will we have created with our customers to ensure success in the marketplace. If that good will is ever breached with our customers, it is hard to recapture. Therefore, it is in our interest to ensure that the goods we sell are produced safely and legally. A reputation gained from decades of good faith efforts to comply with all laws can go down the drain with one widely distributed press story. That is why it is so crucial that Mr. Kernaghan or anyone else churning out press releases or press statements use extreme care when launching public relations attacks and sullying the names of reputable American retail companies without first checking the facts.

Let's take a look at the announcements made by Mr. Kernaghan. In three out of four cases as of the day of his press conference with Congressman Miller and Moran, Mr. Kernaghan had not spoken with anyone at the companies he named as recipients of garments produced at a factory in Choloma, Honduras. I challenge Mr. Kernaghan today to provide private notice to companies when he uncovers a problem and to allow responsible time for corrective action before making his concern or complaints public. Without consultations and communication, retailers and apparel manufacturers are reduced to correcting false impressions created by Mr. Kernaghan and other labor activists through third party media moderators or through Congressional panel dialogues. And while that may make for good theater and use up a lot of press ink, it does nothing to address the real problems of child labor or exploitative labor.

NOTICE AND ACTION

The nation's retailers share the concerns you have expressed with regard to the rights of workers in the apparel industry – whether they live and work in California, New York, New Jersey, El Salvador, Taiwan or Honduras. However, two central questions remain – who is best positioned to ensure the rights of those workers and who has a legal obligation to do so?

In the case of working conditions here in the United States, both the federal government and the various states' governments have an obligation to enforce the laws to the fullest extent possible. Clothing manufacturers are the next line of defense. They have a legal obligation to comply with all applicable laws. As we have discussed with Labor Secretary Robert Reich and his staff, the American retail industry is committed to combating any abuses of our domestic labor laws. In New York, the Federation is sponsoring a compliance seminar to further educate our domestic suppliers of their legal obligations and to underscore our industry's commitment to selling products that are made safely and legally. Similar seminars will be conducted in California and in Texas.

Our commitment extends to the international front as well. U.S. retailers work with foreign suppliers and the national and local governments of those countries to ensure they live by and enforce their own sovereign laws. The international manufacturers, again, represent the first lines of defense, and are charged with obeying all of the laws of the countries where they are doing business. As retailers, we insist in our contracts that the use of child labor or exploitative labor will not be tolerated, and we make unannounced inspection visits to ensure that our products are being made by our contractors in safe and legal environments where workers' rights are protected.

INDUSTRY GUIDELINES

However, the retail industry is active on several other levels to combat the potential use of child labor or exploitative labor. As an industry, we are developing model guidelines and an industry handbook as a means of standardizing industry practices. Here in Washington and in capitals all over the globe, senior executives from the retail industry are meeting with both government and industry officials from our trading partner nations to emphasize our strong concerns about child labor.

We are working with other U.S.-based companies through the U.S. Council for International Business to participate as employers at the International Labor Organization (ILO) in Geneva where Secretary Reich and other labor ministers along with business and union representatives will meet to discuss the global nature of this problem. What they will undoubtedly find – as we have – is that this problem is a very complicated one and one for which overnight solutions do not exist. We urge the committee to move with great care on this very sensitive issue. I assure you that American retailers are willing to play an appropriate role as we all struggle to address the problem of child labor.

TESTIMONY OF KATHIE LEE GIFFORD

Some two months ago I was little more than an entertainer. I associated my name with a line of clothing so that a portion of the dollars raised could go toward helping AIDS and crack-addicted children in New York. That fund raising effort worked beyond my wildest dreams. Today Cody's House and Cassidy's Place have become national models for how to bring sunlight into the lives of children seared by pain. Other charities have also benefited from this effort.

And so it was nothing less than an assault on my very soul, when a witness before Congress suggested that I was using the sweat of children...to help children. I would submit that it was in that single instant that I was introduced to the unforgiving...and

Two girls in the courtyard of the Maurice Sixto Shelter in Haiti, where young domestic workers receive basic education and psychological counselling.

often unfair...cauldron of public policy.

This consumer has learned from people like Wendy Diaz that we are now morally compelled to ask, "What can we do to protect labor rights in factories around the world and right here in America?" Fortunately, there are those seeking to identify and penalize abusers. Wal-Mart, which distributes Kathie Lee fashions, has prevented some 100 factories in 16 countries from working on their garments because of violations. And Wal-Mart is stepping up their oversight in coordination with my own plans for on-site monitoring.

I have discovered that this is not a problem that has cropped up overnight. Experts tell me it is pervasive in the garment industry, and our reports suggest that the sweat shop never really left us. And I am also discovering that there is no one overnight solution to the problem, but we are beginning to create a framework for solutions.

VOLUNTARY MONITORING

For starters, working with Wal-Mart, I plan to implement a plan whereby any Kathie Lee fashion wear will be made in factories willing to submit to surprise inspections by an independent inspector general team. Their mission will be to ensure that safe and responsible working conditions are met. Factories that refuse inspection, or ignore warnings, will be dropped as manufacturers.

And yet, taking work out of factories that abuse their employees puts those employees on unemployment. I would ask this Committee, what "big stick" does the retailer or...the talk show host...have when the only means to get the factory in compliance is moving the work elsewhere.

Ironically, the factory in Honduras where Wendy Diaz was abused continues to employ a steady 1,000 people even after Wal-Mart pulled their work that carries my name. Other manufacturers don't seem to have a problem with reports that these dreadful conditions exist. Punitive actions don't seem to faze the owners of this particular factory.

I have also discovered that implementing an inspector general program is not as simple as hiring a team of investigators. Local laws are often muddy...and following the trail of subcontractors, where much of the abuse takes place, is difficult at best. In addition, employees are often wary of independent inspectors, so decisions have to be made that identify responsible local human rights organizations where there is only one agenda...creating an environment where one can work in dignity. So while an inspector general program is a responsible start, we recognize that it is not a panacea to the problem. It may, in fact, be just the beginning.

SIMPLE IDEAS

I am an entertainer who had a simple idea...create fashion wear with my name on it to help raise money for charity. In hindsight I would conclude that an explanation of quantum physics is far simpler. This much is clear; I have learned that each one of us, whether in Congress, in corporate America, in a television studio, or in a shopping mall, has, as a moral imperative, the need to address this issue.

READING

15

END CHILD LABOR: BAN THEIR PRODUCTS

Christopher H. Smith

Christopher H. Smith represents the 4th District of New Jersey in the United States Congress. Congressman Smith introduced the International Child Labor Elimination Act in the House of Representatives. A hearing was held on this act in the Subcommittee on International Operations and Human Rights on July 26, 1996. The bill was never debated on the House floor.

■ **POINTS TO CONSIDER**

1. Summarize the provisions of the legislation Congressman Smith introduced.

2. Discuss the justification for introducing the legislation.

3. Based upon information in this chapter, how do you evaluate the necessity of this law?

Excerpted from the testimony of Representative Christopher H. Smith before the Subcommittee on International Operations and Human Rights of the House of Representatives Committee on International Relations, June 16, 1996.

This is exactly what we intend to do. In its abusive and coercive forms, child labor is an evil that must be fought as an enemy.

According to the International Labor Organization (ILO), between 100 to 200 million children around the world are being robbed of their childhood for the profit of others. Our inquiry has encountered heartbreaking images of some of them: a three-year-old girl forced to stitch soccer balls for hours on end; children walking barefoot amidst piles of used syringes, removing hypodermic needles in preparation for recycling; boys and girls removed from their homes by abusive masters as human collateral for loans that can never be repaid.

PLIGHT OF CHILDREN

Many of us are parents. Imagine your own children in those circumstances, and you can began to imagine the human misery caused by this exploitation. Even in its less overtly abusive forms, the full time employment of young children denies them the opportunity for basic education, their primary hope of escape from their poverty. It reduces the demand for the labor of adult wage earners, often in areas where there are high rates of adult unemployment. In addition, it allows those who use child workers to profit at the expense of those competitors who have chosen not to exploit this vulnerable source of cheap labor.

BAN THE PRODUCTS

I introduced the International Child Labor Elimination Act – H.R. 3812. This legislation enjoys broad, bipartisan co-sponsorship. Among the co-sponsors are three members of this subcommittee: Congressmen Henry Hyde, Tom Lantos, and Jim Moran. Other original co-sponsors of the legislation include Congresswoman Ileana Ros-Lehtinen of Florida and Congressman Joe Kennedy of Massachusetts. This legislation will turn our conscientious concern into an engine for international human rights reform – using all the tools at the disposal of the government of the United States.

— *First,* it will ban the import of products made by child labor.

— *Second,* it will prohibit foreign aid, other than humanitarian aid, to countries that do not have or do not enforce child labor laws.

Nearly a third of the agricultural workforce in some developing countries is made up of children, according to a recent ILO report. This young cane cutter is one of millions of children under the age of 14 working in Brazil.

UNICEF/Huzak

– *Third*, it will prohibit loans from United States bilateral lending agencies to businesses or projects that use child labor, and will direct our representatives to the World Bank and other multilateral institutions to oppose the provision of funds to industries that use child labor.

– *Last* but not least, it will provide needed funding – $50 million over five years – to the International Program on the Elimination of Child Labor (IPEC) of the International Labor Organization. So far, the United States has contributed only $3.6 million to this program. Germany, the largest contributor, has donated $65 million. Even Spain, whose economy and national budget are far smaller than those of the United States, has contributed $12.5 million, almost four times the amount we have provided. I was shocked and disappointed to learn that the United States is not paying its fair share to this comprehensive and promising effort to end child labor – indeed, the Administration's budget request does not even suggest that Congress authorize these funds. Obviously, it is not enough to make a contribution to an international program. We must do far more. But it is a beginning, and it is long overdue.

HUMAN RIGHTS AND PROFITEERING

Pope John Paul II discussed the plight of children in various parts of the world, and challenged governments "to intervene strongly...against those who harm and scandalize the most defenseless among us." In his words, governments must act "with all the force of law" to stop the exploitation of children. This is exactly what we intend to do. In its abusive and coercive forms, child labor is an evil that must be fought as an enemy. It is time to

109

join the battle, and to fight for these forgotten children. When the International Child Labor Elimination Act becomes law, countries and companies will no longer be able to profit by neglecting the internationally recognized human rights of the most vulnerable people on earth.

THE INTERNATIONAL CHILD LABOR ELIMINATION ACT

Introduced by Rep. Christopher Smith (R.-N.J.) with co-sponsors.

Section-by-Section Summary Analysis

Section (1) Short Title.

Section (2) Findings describe the nature and scope of the child labor problem, and applicable international conventions and standards.

Section (3) Requires that the Secretary of Labor annually identify countries that do not prohibit child labor, or that do not effectively enforce their child labor laws, and industries within those countries that use child labor. If warranted by new information or a change in the laws or practices of an identified country, the Secretary may revoke such an identification at any time. A specific company that would otherwise be included within an identification may be exempted from the Act's sanctions if the Secretary is satisfied that no goods produced by that company are products of child labor.

Section (4) Prohibits the import of products manufactured in countries and industries identified under Section (3).

Section (5) Prohibits United States assistance – except for humanitarian aid – to countries identified under Section (3). Requires that United States representatives to multilateral lending institutions oppose loans and other subsidies to or for any industry identified under Section (3). Allows the President to exempt countries and industries from this prohibition if the exemption is necessary to the vital national interests of the United States.

Section (6) Outlines civil and criminal penalties for violation of this Act.

Section (7) Charges the President with issuing such regulations as are necessary to carry out this Act.

Section (8) Authorizes the appropriation of a $10 million contribution in each of the next five fiscal years to the International Program on the Elimination of Child Labor (IPEC) of the International Labor Organization.

Section (9) Defines "child labor" as (a) work by children below either the age at which they complete compulsory schooling or 15 years of age, whichever is less, except for part-time work by children 14 or older that does not interfere with their health or education; or (b) work by children under 18 that would be likely to jeopardize the health, safety, or morals of a young person. Defines other terms used in this Act.

Excerpted from the Summary of H.R. 3182, The International Child Labor Elimination Act.

END CHILD LABOR: BUY THEIR PRODUCTS

William Anderson

William Anderson wrote the following for The Free Market. *Anderson is a graduate student in Economics at Auburn University in Auburn, Alabama.* The Free Market *is a publication of the Ludwig von Mises Institute, Auburn, Alabama.*

■ POINTS TO CONSIDER

1. What role does the author believe labor unions play in the child labor debate?

2. Evaluate the author's defense of factory conditions in developing nations.

3. Discuss the "lessons from the past" employed in the article.

4. The article suggests a solution to "improve the lot of Third World children." Do you agree with this? Explain.

William Anderson, "Kathie Lee's Children," **The Free Market**, September 1996: 1, 7.

***With a booming international market for clothing,
factories have sprung up all over to offer a way out of
poverty and disease.***

Media personality Kathie Lee Gifford took quite a pounding
when the National Labor Committee, a labor union organization,
found that some of the clothes sold under her label in the U.S.
were made by children in a Honduran "sweat shop."

Union lobbyists and their paid-for politicians paraded 15-year-
old Wendy Diaz around Washington to testify about how badly
the factory had treated her: long hours, few bathroom breaks, and
31 cents an hour. The unions then insisted that no more clothing
be imported from this factory, or any similar one.

SOCIALIST AGENDA

Gifford, now properly contrite, has devoted her life to ending
child labor. She backs the UN's International Labor Organization
bid for U.S. subsidies to enforce a global ban on employing young
people, and otherwise implement its socialist charter. Gifford also
promises to donate the profits from her clothing line, now made
only by adults, to a myriad of liberal causes.

A few days after the Gifford story broke, the unions took advantage of the attention and stepped up their campaign. They said
that basketball shoes bearing the name of Michael Jordan were
made by overseas children making even less than Kathie Lee's
kids.

But the story did not take off. The reason: Nike fought back. It
pointed out that the workers in Pakistan who make Nike products
earn five times the pay of other workers in that country. Far from
exploiting children, Nike is actually doing the workers of Pakistan
a great service.

RELATIVE SUCCESS

Basic economic logic explains why. If young people and their
families in the Third World would be better off idle, they would
stop working. If they could get higher wages for the same work,
they would change jobs. If they could make a better investment in
their future in some other way, they would do so. As it stands,
however, these supposed "sweat shops" are the best thing that's

A girl in Niger goes about her chores.

happened to the Third World in decades.

Let's return to the Gifford case. Ten years ago, Honduras had virtually no assembly plants. But with a booming international market for clothing, factories have sprung up all over the country to offer a way out of poverty and disease. Today, the country has 160 assembly plants that employ some 75,000 people.

Those lucky enough to work in these factories are doing well in a country where per capita income is $600 a year and unemployment is 40 percent. Plants routinely subsidize lunch, offer free medical care to employees, and are air conditioned – benefits unheard of in other lines of employment.

As one worker told the *New York Times,* "This has been an enormous advance for me, and I give thanks to the *maquila* [factory] for it. My monthly income is seven times what I made in the countryside, and I've gained 30 pounds since I started working here."

LABOR CHOICES

The labor force is extremely fluid, bid from factory to factory at ever-higher wages. If a worker doesn't like the terms, he goes elsewhere. The owners try to make their working conditions better to attract the best employees. As factories invest more, and workers become more productive, they command a higher wage. Already, wages are on the rise in Honduras.

The denunciation of child labor assumes people in Honduras have the option of keeping their children fed and idle for 18 years. But this is fantasy. As Wendy Diaz herself said, she worked long hours to provide food and clothing for her two younger brothers, who might otherwise have starved.

Late in the day, she even urged the U.S. not to cut off trade, for fear the factories would have to shut down and her friends would be forced into prostitution. But the damage was already done: frightened by the U.S. media campaign, her former factory started laying off workers under 16 and stopped hiring altogether.

VICTORIAN REALITIES

The issue of child labor is hardly new. In 1802, the British Parliament passed the first law against child labor in factories. It was the beginning of a legislative process that continues well into this century. Historians usually portray anti-child labor crusaders as humanitarians. On the contrary, they succeeded only in cutting off economic opportunity, and making children less valuable to their parents.

The pre-factory age was not a time of happy, contented kids. From 1730 to 1740, 75 percent of children in England died before age five. From 1810 to 1829, supposedly the evil age of the factory, infant mortality fell to 32 percent and would continue to drop. Capitalism and the industrial revolution gave youngsters a chance to survive.

Nassau Senior, one of the great British economists of the mid-1800s, noted that most of the agitation for the anti-child labor Factory Acts came not from humanitarians, but from organizations of adults who wanted more textile work for themselves. "They got up therefore a frightful, and (as far as we have heard and seen) an utterly unfounded picture of the ill treatment of the children," Senior wrote.

PROTECTIONISM PERSISTS

So it is today. American labor unions and their allies paint a horrific picture, and they offer a theory of economics to back it up: by purchasing products made by exploited youngsters, American consumers are forcing them into a living Hell. Stop buying the products, make them in the U.S. instead, and the children will be free to play and go to school.

Factory owners in Bangladesh once faced international sanctions unless they stopped using child labor. Oxfam, the British charity, reported that the factories laid off 30,000 child workers. The children then took more dangerous jobs, with thousands becoming prostitutes or starving.

Like their English counterparts of 150 years ago, the unions who pinned Ms. Gifford to the wall have a dark, hidden agenda. Their goal is not to help children; it is to cut off imports, rip off American consumers, and pad their own wages at everyone else's expense. They have no plans for dealing with the problems of Honduras's children after they've been sent packing. As a union official shrugged to the *New York Times,* "I'm not an economist."

Ironically, when we hear accusations of child labor in Honduras, Pakistan, and Bangladesh, it's a sign that these countries are on the right track. It suggests they are becoming competitive with monopolistic unions here. But instead of competing fair and square, the unions turn to protectionist politics and media propaganda. The best way to improve the lot of Third World children is not to boycott, but to buy the products of their labors. It is the old Kathie Lee Gifford, not the new and improved one, who is the real humanitarian.

INTERPRETING EDITORIAL CARTOONS

This activity may be used as an individualized study guide for students in libraries and resource centers or as a discussion catalyst in small group and classroom discussions.

Although cartoons are usually humorous, the main intent of most political cartoonists is not to entertain. Cartoons express serious social comment about important issues. Using graphic and visual arts, the cartoonist expresses opinions and attitudes. By employing an entertaining and often light-hearted visual format, cartoonists may have as much or more impact on national and world issues as editorial and syndicated columnists.

■ **POINTS TO CONSIDER**

1. Examine the cartoon on page 25.

2. How would you describe the message of the cartoon? Try to describe the message in one to three sentences.

3. Do you agree with the message expressed in the cartoon? Why or why not?

4. Are any of the readings in Chapter Two in basic agreement with the cartoon?

CHAPTER 3

THE GLOBAL ECONOMY: ECONOMIC GROWTH AND HUMAN RIGHTS

17. INTERNATIONAL LABOR STANDARDS: 118
    THE POINT
    Neil Kearney

18. INTERNATIONAL LABOR STANDARDS: 125
    THE COUNTERPOINT
    Jagdish Bhagwati

19. MOST FAVORED NATION TRADE STATUS   131
    WILL PROMOTE PROGRESS IN CHINA
    Madeleine K. Albright

20. MOST FAVORED NATION STATUS   136
    MUST BE DENIED
    Representative Richard A. Gephardt

21. THE NORTH AMERICAN FREE TRADE AGREEMENT: 142
    A SUCCESS
    The Clinton Administration

22. THE NORTH AMERICAN FREE TRADE AGREEMENT: 148
    A FAILED EXPERIMENT
    Economic Policy Institute, et al.

23. ENDLESS GROWTH IS OBSOLETE   156

24. GLOBALIZATION LEADS TO PROGRESS   164
    Thomas d'Aquino

READING

17

INTERNATIONAL LABOR STANDARDS: THE POINT

Neil Kearney

Neil Kearney represents the International Textile, Garment and Leather Workers Federation, an international federation which is the umbrella for 180 trade union organizations in 85 countries.

◼ POINTS TO CONSIDER

1. According to Kearney, what is happening to wages with further economic globalization?

2. Explain future consequences of current child labor practices.

3. Summarize current international labor guidelines, their implementation, and enforcement.

4. Define the Social Clause and discuss how it can be employed.

Excerpted from the testimony of Neil Kearney before the Subcommittee on Labor of the House of Representatives Committee on Labor and Human Resources, September 21, 1994.

The best way of combating child labor would be to link trade and worker rights.

Nobody really knows the number of children in full-time employment across the world. The most commonly cited range is from 80 to 200 million. Even 200 million probably understates the reality. In Asia alone there are tens of millions of them, victims of a virtual slave trade taking place in total impunity under the nose of sometimes indifferent and often powerless governments. A few years ago, the International Labor Organization (ILO) estimated that in China alone, there were 40 million working children, aged between 10 and 14. But Asia does not have the monopoly on child labor: Brazil alone has an estimated seven million children at work. Child labor is also growing in the United States and in Europe, regions where it had been almost eliminated.

THE HORROR OF CHILD LABOR

Enough can never be said or written about the evil of child labor. Far too many people try to ignore this brutalization of children, thinking that because it is in some other country it can be forgotten, or even when it is on the doorstep that it is the inevitable consequence of poverty and thus impossible to really tackle.

The following are a few examples of the horror inflicted on millions of children around the world. These are not images drawn from a fevered imagination. They are day-to-day occurrences involving children in the textile, carpet, garment, and leather industries. In every case mentioned, the employers involved were producing for multinational companies.

In one carpet factory in Karah, Pakistan, 300 children, some as young as five, work alongside each other from 6 in the morning to 7 at night for less than 20 cents a day. A sign on the wall says any child caught sleeping will be fined US$60. If they cry for their mothers they are beaten with sticks, chains and carpet forks. Some have spent up to four or five days chained to the loom at which they work because of some indiscretion, often just a mistake in the weaving. One boy, ill and unable to work for two days, was forcefully brought to the weaving shed by the owner and hung from a ceiling fan for two days.

In India, many are branded to indicate the owner to whom they belong; others have been hung upside-down from trees as a punishment for trying to escape. In Delhi, an 11-year-old had paraffin poured over him and was set alight by his boss for asking for time off. In Bangladesh, I have seen nine-year-olds working three days around the clock sewing shirts, being allowed only a couple of one-hour breaks to sleep next to their machines.

SMALL HANDS MAKE BIG PROFITS

The question is often asked why governments in developing countries don't do more to protect children from such exploitation. One reason is that, sadly, far too many governments are indifferent to the problem, if not downright implicated in its expansion, believing that rock-bottom wages and appalling working conditions are the only way to prosperity.

Another reason is that intense competition among developing countries is pitting country against country in the battle to secure a limited share of world markets, thus pushing down wages and working conditions for the workers concerned.

Pressure from unscrupulous wholesalers and retailers in the West is another factor that is further impoverishing poor countries. Buyers are pushing down export prices, forcing local producers to cut costs by employing children, who generally earn one-third to one-tenth of the wages of an adult worker.

GLOBALIZATION

As the textile, clothing and leather industries have globalized, child labor has multiplied. The prospects of ever larger mark-ups send companies in search of even lower wages, and children are, of course, cheap and dispensable. Sometimes unbelievably so. When I asked one Karachi textile manufacturer about children working in his mill, he brushed aside my question with the remark: "I take anyone who can work, young, middle-aged, old. If a 10-year-old can do the job, I will take him. And I don't care if he's dead in a fortnight."

Goods produced by children in conditions of virtual serfdom for the stores of North America, Europe, Japan and the rest of the industrialized world don't come cheap for the consumer. For example, five-year-olds working 15 hours a day in Nepal's carpet export industry earn perhaps US$ 25 for a carpet that will retail at up to US$ 4,000 in the United States or Europe. And the wage

"A Ship!"

costs in a US$ 60 shirt bought in the U.S. are often less than 10 cents.

TOMORROW'S UNEMPLOYED ADULTS

The employment of children is of course a crime against the children themselves. A recent study on Pakistan's carpet factories estimated that 50,000 children in forced labor in this sector will die before their twelfth birthday from malnutrition and disease.

And what about those who survive? Take away the formative years of childhood, and one wonders what the end result will be. How will these children be able to function as adults, and what contribution will they be able to make to society in general? What socially incompetent and emotionally crippled young people is today's world guilty of producing?

These children become gradually unemployable as adults because of illness – health hazards which affect children to an ever greater extent – or because they lack proper vocational training, which means that their own children will, in turn, be forced to work.

But child labor is also a crime against adult workers employed in the industry, because it undermines job security and drives down the wages and working conditions of adult workers. In this competition, wages are often so reduced that the combined earnings of the parents and the child are less than the wage of one parent before. From the purely economic point of view alone, it is disastrous to send children out to work.

Take Bangladesh, for instance. Estimates suggest that between 25 and 30% of all workers in the garment industry are under 14. In some factories, the figure is as high as 70%. Women seeking employment are often asked if they have any children who could work. If they don't, they are then invited to take the job at the child rate. As a consequence, wages in the industry have dropped from US$30 per month to around US$10 in many factories.

ELIMINATE CHILD LABOR?

International conventions exist on child labor. In 1973, the ILO adopted Convention No. 138, which sets the minimum age for employment at 15 as a general rule and 14 for countries whose economy and educational facilities are insufficiently developed. Unfortunately, most nations have not ratified that Convention, and even among those who ratified it, some are not enforcing it. The ILO itself has no power to enforce its conventions, and it is up to individual countries to put teeth into the standards contained in the conventions. This rarely happens, and that's why other action is also needed to ensure that real measures are taken against child slavery.

THE SOCIAL CLAUSE

The best way of combating child labor would be to link trade and worker rights through the inclusion of a Social Clause in international trade agreements. The Social Clause would say that countries which are willfully suppressing basic worker rights in order to gain an advantage over competing countries should not be allowed to participate in world trade. This would render access to world markets dependent on a country accepting and implementing some basic labor standards, including the non-use of child labor, the right to form trade unions, the right to bargain collectively, and a ban on the use of forced labor and discrimination.

REDEFINING DEVELOPMENT

What is fundamentally at issue is a change in the way we conceive development. To date, it has been narrowly defined as capital accumulation, with some concessions to the need for investment in the human resources of a country as a means of improving its economic efficiency and attractiveness for foreign investment. The issue of enhancing worker rights goes to the question of equity: who gains and who loses in the process of development. It is time to redress the imbalance, which in poor nations has favored the interests of capital to the disadvantage of working people.

Excerpted from the testimony of Jerome I. Levinson before the Subcommittee on International Development, Finance, Trade and Monetary Policy of the House of Representatives Committee on Banking, Finance and Urban Affairs, June 28, 1994.

The trade union proposal is that the Social Clause would be implemented through the same transparent procedures that govern all of international trade through the General Agreement on Trade and Tariffs (GATT) and its successor the World Trade Organization (WTO). An ILO/WTO Advisory Board would need to be set up to review the basis of specific complaints to see whether WTO member states were observing specified minimum labor standards. If a country were found to be systematically disregarding those standards, the Advisory Board would recommend measures to be taken within a specified period of time, and the ILO would offer technical assistance. Of course, change could not be expected overnight, and trade sanctions would only be triggered for blatant disregard of minimum standards by a government.

A Social Clause would not act – as some have claimed – as a means of controlling imports or establishing barriers to trade – but as a positive lever to improve working conditions in exporting countries. It would establish the most basic of employment standards.

Most countries would have nothing to fear from such a clause. On the contrary, they have everything to gain, as the Social Clause would promote fair competition between developing country exporters and would ensure that those who do respect minimum standards are not penalized for their efforts to eradicate child labor. The benefits of trade would thus be distributed more fairly within the producing countries, ultimately benefitting their own growth and the expansion of world trade generally.

BAN IMPORTS MADE BY CHILD LABOR

Governments must legislate in a way which deals with manufacturers, wholesalers and retailers in the only way they understand – economically. These groups have ignored the moral arguments and the appeals to national interest; now they must risk losing access to lucrative markets. Legislation should provide for importers who intentionally violate the law to be subjected to punitive fines and terms of imprisonment. In cases where it is found that child labor was used, products from the entire industry in a particular country should be banned. Such legislation would create a strong incentive for industry to police itself and to ensure that its access to markets is not endangered.

CONSUMER PRESSURE

Consumers play a major role in forcing companies to rethink their policies. Today, more and more companies are realizing that consumers are not only interested in the products they buy but are also concerned about the conditions under which products are manufactured. In response to consumer pressure, a number of companies, particularly in the United States, are establishing corporate codes of conduct for their buyers, suppliers and contractors, as well as instituting new procedures for auditing their imports.

PROVISION OF EDUCATION

Children belong in school, not in factories. But parents in poor countries often cannot afford to allow their children time off from work to attend school, because they themselves are unemployed or because their wages have been so reduced that the combined earnings of parents and children are less than the wage of one parent before!

The most important instrument for ensuring that children do not work is to have them attend school. But the reality is that sometimes there are no schools. Therefore, increased resources need to be allocated to education, including school lunch programs and the elimination of school fees and other student costs. This also means finding other ways to make sure that school enrollment for children of the poorest families is not an impossible liability.

READING

18

INTERNATIONAL LABOR STANDARDS: THE COUNTERPOINT

Jagdish Bhagwati

Jagdish Bhagwati is the Arthur Lehman Professor of Economics and Professor of Political Science at Columbia University. He is the former Economic Policy Advisor to the Director General, General Agreement on Trade and Tariffs (GATT) and the author of Protectionism *and* The World Trading System at Risk.

■ POINTS TO CONSIDER

1. Bhagwati suggests why labor cannot be protected through the WTO in the same way as intellectual property. Explain.

2. Discuss the motives behind those who support the Social Clause, according to the article. What traditional coalitions or lines are drawn?

3. Why is the idea of international labor standards difficult?

Excerpted from the testimony of Jagdish Bhagwati before the Subcommittee on International Development, Finance, Trade and Monetary Policy of the House of Representatives Committee on Banking, Finance and Urban Affairs, June 24, 1994.

The reality is that diversity of labor practices and standards is widespread in practice and reflects, not necessarily venality and wickedness, but rather diversity of cultural values, economic conditions and analytical beliefs.

The linkage between "labor rights" and international trade, such that a country's access to external markets is to be made conditional in some fashion on the acceptability of that country's internal "labor standards," is now a matter on the international agenda. The objective is the enactment of a Social Clause, specifying Labor Standards as pre-conditions for market access rights by the World Trade Organization (WTO).

The question is already divisive, pitting most economists against the labor union activists and their political allies, and certainly the more articulate developing countries (the South) against the developed countries (the North). The question has the potential of frustrating the WTO's essential purpose of providing an overall framework for liberal trade rules by encouraging protectionist misuse of trade rules instead. It is also resurrecting the North-South divide that afflicted the world economy in the late 1970s. The issue therefore needs to be carefully and dispassionately examined before decisions are taken in the forthcoming months.

COMMON FALLACIES

At the outset, fallacies current in some of the discussion in the United States must be examined. Labor spokesmen commonly argue that WTO has accepted safeguards for "capital" and multinationals in shape of trade rules, investment rules and Intellectual Property Protection; why not adopt rules for labor?

But this argument forgets that the trade rules are for economic efficiency, which generally helps everyone (with internal distributional problems being tackled by other policies); they are not there simply to assist specific factors of production (i.e., capital) or economic agents (i.e., multinationals), as such. Besides, rules about intellectual property protection, while different in essential respects in economic logic from those regarding trade, do have some essential trade aspects: the transfer and diffusion of technology, and payments for the same, across countries can be legitimately viewed as international trade in technology, whereas no such case can be made for "labor standards."

126

Free trade promotes economic efficiency and maximizes national income; its distributional impact is addressed by other domestic policies (such as adjustment assistance, retraining programs, progressive income taxation, etc.)

MORAL SUPERIORITY

Moreover, the matter is often presented as demonstrating US "moral leadership," in a unique and characteristic way that other nations generally cannot provide. But, even if we agree that the United States has often taken the moral lead in questions of worldwide importance, this does not automatically imply that the Social Clause initiative reflects, in a deep way, broad moral concerns rather than the narrow economic interests of specific groups. Nor should we regard the many who oppose such initiatives as morally defective simply because those who propose them claim the higher moral ground.

Deep scrutiny of the Social Clause initiative, its desirability and its possible design, cannot be avoided, especially if its economic consequence was to impose inappropriate labor practices on poor countries or to jeopardize their trade access if they resisted them. Either way, a Social Clause could hurt their prospects for efficiency and growth, and adversely affect in consequence the goal of poverty eradication, making the Social Clause a morally defective, rather than a morally superior, innovation.

THE REAL ARGUMENT

Central to American thinking on the question of the Social Clause is the notion that competitive advantage can sometimes be "illegitimate." In particular, it is argued that if labor standards elsewhere are different and unacceptable morally, then the resulting competition is illegitimate and unfair.

When this argument is made about a practice such as slavery (defined strictly as the practice of owning and transacting in human beings, as in the centuries before the Abolitionists triumphed), there will be nearly universal agreement that if slavery produces competitive advantage, that advantage is illegitimate and ought to be rejected.

This argument can be purely moral: e.g., that we will not profit from the fruits of slavery, since it implies our complicity in the practice. But the politically more salient argument is one of "competitiveness": that it imposes an adjustment cost on our import-competing industries that is illegitimate and therefore "unfair."

The real problem with this argument, however, is that universally condemned practices such as slavery are rare indeed. True, the International Labor Organization (ILO) has many Conventions that many nations have signed. But many have been signed simply because in effect they are not binding.

DIVERSE CULTURES

Indeed, the reality is that diversity of labor practices and standards is widespread in practice and reflects, not necessarily venality and wickedness, but rather diversity of cultural values, economic conditions and analytical beliefs and theories concerning the economic (and therefore moral) consequences of specific labor standards. The notion that labor standards can be universalized, like human rights such as liberty and *habeas corpus,* simply by calling them "labor rights" ignores the fact that this easy equation between culture-specific labor standards and universal human rights cannot survive deeper scrutiny.

Take the United States itself. Worker participation in decision-making on the plant is more widespread in Europe than in North America: are we to then condemn North America to denial of trading rights by the Europeans? Migrant labor is ill-treated in US agriculture due to inadequate enforcement, if investigative television shows are a guide; does this mean other nations should prohibit the import of US agricultural products? Even the right to organize trade unions may be considered to be inadequate in the US if we go by "results," as the US favors in judging Japan: less than 20% of the US labor force is unionized. Strikes in essential industries are restricted: but the definition of such industries also reflects economic structure and political realities, making the US definition only culture-specific and hence open to objection by others.

CHILD LABOR

Even the developing country phenomena such as the use of child labor raise complex questions (as indeed recognized by the ILO, though not in the arguments heard in the United States today). The use of child labor, as such, is surely not the issue. Few children grow up even in the US without working as babysitters or delivering newspapers; many are even paid by parents for house-work in the home. The pertinent social question is rather whether children at work are protected from hazardous conditions. In real-ity, this problem applies to a rare few industries (e.g., glassmak-ing), contrary to the assertions often made.

Whether child labor should be altogether prohibited in a poor country is a matter on which views legitimately differ. Many feel that children's work is unavoidable in the face of poverty and that the alternative to it is starvation which is a greater calamity, and that eliminating child labor would then be like voting to eliminate abortion without worrying about the needs of the children that are then born.

Insisting on the "positive rights"-related right to unionize to demand higher wages, for instance, as against the "negative rights"-related right of freedom to associate for political activity, for example, also can be morally obtuse. In practice, such a right could imply higher wages for the "insiders" who have jobs, at the expense of the unemployed "outsiders." Besides, the unions in developing countries with large populations and much poverty are likely to be in the urban-industrial activities, with the industri-al proletariat among the better-off sections of the population, whereas the real poverty is among the nonunionized landless labor. Raising the wages of the former will generally hurt, in the opinion of many developing-country economists, the prospects of rapid accumulation and growth which alone can pull more of the landless labor eventually into gainful employment. If so, the impo-sition of the culture-specific developed-country-union views on poor countries about the rights of unions to push for higher wages will resolve current equity and intergenerational equity problems in ways that are morally unacceptable to these countries, and correctly so.

FEARS AND FALLACIES

One is then led to conclude that the idea of the Social Clause in the WTO is rooted generally in an ill-considered rejection of the general legitimacy of diversity of labor standards and practices across countries. Wittingly or unwittingly, its proposed contents are also selectively focused currently on the practices of the developing countries, shielding the practices of the developed countries: those throwing stones at other people's glass houses have put fortresses around their own. Thus, the alleged claim for the universality of labor standards is (except for a rare few cases such as slavery) generally unpersuasive; and the proponents of that view are inconsistent in turning their attention and political activism only to practices of countries in economic competition with their own, instead of looking at labor practices on their own turf.

The developing countries cannot then be blamed for worrying that the recent escalation of support for such a Clause in the WTO in major countries derives instead from the desire of labor unions to protect their jobs by protecting the industries that face competition from the poor countries. They fear that moral arguments are produced to justify restrictions on such trade since they are so effective in the public domain. In short, the "white man's burden" is being exploited to secure the "white man's gain." Or, to use another metaphor, "blue protectionism" is breaking out, masked behind a moral facade.

In fact, the salience which the Social Clause crusade has acquired in the US and Europe owes much to the widespread fear, evident during the North American Free Trade Agreement (NAFTA) debate in the United States, that trade with the poor countries (with abundant unskilled labor) will produce unemployment and reductions in the real wages of the unskilled in the rich countries. The Social Clause is, in this perspective, a way in which the fearful unions seek to raise the costs of production in the poor countries as free trade with them threatens their jobs and wages. That this fear is unjustified by recent extensive analyses of the problem by economists does not reduce its potency in fuelling the demands for the Social Clause.

READING

19

MOST FAVORED NATION TRADE STATUS WILL PROMOTE PROGRESS IN CHINA

Madeleine K. Albright

Madeleine K. Albright is Secretary of State for the Clinton Administration. She is the first woman appointed to the office.

■ **POINTS TO CONSIDER**

1. Discuss the many diplomatic changes that have occurred between the U.S. and China.

2. What does "Most Favored Nation" (MFN) trade status mean?

3. Summarize how the author characterizes China's human rights record.

4. Explain the potential consequences, according to Albright, of revoking MFN for China.

Excerpted from the testimony of Madeleine K. Albright before the Senate Finance Committee, June 10, 1997.

There is no greater opportunity – or challenge – in U.S. foreign policy today than to encourage China's integration as a fully responsible member of the international system.

We now have an unprecedented opportunity to integrate the world around basic principles of democracy, open markets, law and a common commitment to peace.

It is in America's interests to strengthen the system, to ensure that it is based on high standards and sound principles of law, and to make it more inclusive. We do this by helping transitional states to play a greater role, by giving a boost to the weak states most willing to help themselves, and by making it clear to the outlaw states that they cannot prosper at the expense of the rest; they must either reform or suffer in isolation. There is no greater opportunity – or challenge – in U.S. foreign policy today than to encourage China's integration as a fully responsible member of the international system. President Clinton's decision to extend Most Favored Nation (MFN) or normal trade relations with China reflects our commitment to this goal.

Principled criticism of Chinese actions that offend our values or run counter to our interests is vital – because it demonstrates that the concerns we address through our diplomacy are deeply rooted in the convictions of the American people. We believe that America's leadership in Asia and our interests in China – including Hong Kong – can best be advanced by continuing to engage Chinese leaders on a wide range of security, economic and political issues. This would not be possible if we revoked MFN.

REGIONAL INTERESTS

America is and will remain an Asia-Pacific power. In a region where we have fought three wars in the last half-century, our role continues to be vital – from the stabilizing effects of our diplomatic and military presence, to the galvanizing impact of our commercial ties, to the transforming influence of our ideals. Our commitment is solid because it is solidly based on American interests.

Because of China's relative weakness for the past several centuries, its emergence as a modern power is a major historical event. Indeed, no nation will play a larger role in shaping the course of 21st-century Asia. Already, China affects America's vital interests across the board.

China possesses nuclear weapons and the world's largest standing army. It also has a rapidly advancing industrial and technological capacity. And it seeks to re-unify its national territory and settle its contested borders with its neighbors. For all these reasons, China affects our core security interests: the nonproliferation of weapons of mass destruction; the protection of sea lanes in the Pacific and Indian Oceans; the stability of the Korean Peninsula; and the peaceful resolution of issues between Taiwan and the Peoples' Republic of China (PRC).

ECONOMY

The Chinese economy is already one of the largest in the world, and many observers predict that if China's current growth rates continue, it will be the largest within several decades. Therefore, China affects our primary economic interest in expanding American exports and creating a more open global trade and investment regime in the coming century.

With its 1.2 billion people rapidly modernizing, China will have a huge impact on the environment. In addition, China borders on the world's largest opium-producing areas, and it is a potentially huge source of human migration. That is why China affects our urgent global interests in preventing environmental degradation and in combating terrorism, narcotics and alien smuggling.

Although China is undeniably more open today than two decades ago, its people still lack basic civil and political liberties. The manner in which China is governed affects virtually all of our security and economic interests in the region as well as our abiding interest in promoting respect for universally recognized standards of tolerance and law.

THE CHALLENGE

The fundamental challenge for U.S. policy is to persuade China to define its own national interests in a manner compatible with ours. That's why we are working to encourage China's development as a secure, prosperous and open society as well as its integration as a full and responsible member of the international community.

In so doing, we have not acquiesced to Chinese violations of international norms – and we will not. On the contrary, we have taken determined actions to curb such violations and to protect our interests.

For example, the United States continues to be concerned about Chinese sales of dangerous weapons and technologies. The United States has also contributed to a lessening of tensions in the Taiwan Strait. In the economic area, we have made progress in opening China's markets. In 1996, in response to China's inadequate implementation of an agreement to protect U.S. intellectual property (including music, videos and software), President Clinton prepared to apply tariffs of 100% on $2 billion of Chinese exports to the United States. The President's action led to an important follow-up accord providing more effective protection for our intellectual property and expanded access to our movies and videos. During the past year, China has taken strong measures to implement this agreement, seizing 10 million pirated disks, closing some 40 illegal CD factories and establishing hot-lines that are offering rewards 20 times the size of the average annual wage for tips leading to the closing of such a factory.

We have also advanced negotiations on China's accession to the World Trade Organization (WTO). We have worked closely with China to identify the steps it must take to broaden access to its markets and bring its trade practices into line with WTO rules. Our combination of rigorous entry criteria and generous technical assistance has paid off. Although differences remain in the negotiations and the outcome remains uncertain, China has become increasingly serious in the proposals it has put forward, and is coming to understand that membership is not a right but a privilege accompanied by responsibilities.

In the environmental field, our two governments have increased our cooperation by establishing the U.S.-China Environment and Development Forum. Vice President Gore inaugurated the Forum during his recent visit to China. The Forum has set an ambitious agenda for collaboration in four areas: energy policy, environmental policy, science for sustainable development, and commercial cooperation. The combined efforts of our two Environmental Protection Agencies have already resulted in China's recent decision to eliminate the use of leaded gas and in the undertaking of joint studies on the health effects of air pollution.

HUMAN RIGHTS

In human rights, overall progress has been hard to quantify. On

PROMOTING DEMOCRACY

Born in the so-called Great Cultural Revolution, I and my fellow students in the Tiananmen Student Movement came of age in the years when China had to adopt the Open Door policy for economic development. When trade brought our eyes beyond China's borders, we were shocked by the huge discrepancies between China's overwhelming poverty and the high-quality standard of living in the West, and we began to challenge the dreams depicted long ago by the communist party.

Intellectuals and students of our generation began the journey to explore real solutions to China's problems. In the early 1980s, trade with the West also brought to China a flood of information. And the political philosophy of many leading Chinese dissidents, including myself and many of my colleagues in the Tiananmen Student Movement, was derived from this open era in China.

Excerpted from the testimony of Nick Liang before the Senate Committee on Finance, June 10, 1997.

the one hand, China's exposure to the outside world has brought increased openness, social mobility, choice of employment and access to information. On the other hand, as we have documented in our annual human rights report, China's official practices still fall far short of internationally accepted standards.

It is our hope that the trend towards greater economic and social integration of China will have a liberalizing effect on political and human rights practices. Given the nature of the Chinese government, that progress will be gradual, at best, and is by no means inevitable.

However, economic openness can create conditions that brave men and women dedicated to freedom can take advantage of to seek change. It diminishes the arbitrary power of the state over the day to day lives of its people. It strengthens the demand for the rule of law. It raises popular expectations. And it exposes millions of people to the simple, powerful idea that a better way of life is possible.

READING

20

MOST FAVORED NATION STATUS MUST BE DENIED

Representative Richard A. Gephardt

Richard A. Gephardt is the minority leader in the House of Representatives. He is a Democrat serving the Third Congressional District of Missouri.

■ POINTS TO CONSIDER

1. Explain Gephardt's view of the human rights situation in China.

2. Define the speaker's view on Most Favored Nation (MFN) trade status for China. Explain why the speaker takes this position.

3. Discuss Gephardt's view of the U.S. role as a trading nation. Compare and/or contrast this with what the author contends were past policy objectives.

4. How does the author respond to his critics?

Excerpted from the address of Congressman Richard A. Gephardt before the Detroit Economic Club, May 27, 1997.

The repression of political rights is inevitably combined with the denial of economic rights.

CONTINUING STRUGGLE FOR FREEDOM

Today one of the defenders of America is a Chinese electrician named Wei Jingsheng. In 1978, Wei displayed a poster on a brick wall in Xidan. On it he wrote, "The result of all struggle involving the people's resistance to oppression and exploitation is determined by their success or failure in obtaining democracy!" A few months later, after writing another essay, he was arrested, convicted and sentenced to 15 years in prison. He languished there until September of 1993 when he was released six months early, just as China was mounting an all-out campaign to host the 2000 Olympics.

In 1995, a year in which he was nominated for the Nobel Peace Prize, Wei was formally charged with attempting to overthrow the government. After a six hour trial, he was sentenced to prison for fourteen more years. Today he is being kept in an unheated cell with bright lights glaring 24 hours a day. He is behind bars, but like Solzhenitsyn and Mandela, his spirit is unbroken. In a letter written from his prison cell to Chinese leaders, Wei said that human rights "are common objective standards which apply to all governments and all individuals...Like objective existence and objective laws, they are objective truths. That was why Rousseau called them 'natural rights'."

The family of free nations has expanded – and this should make us redouble our commitment to the world-wide victory of democracy. This is the great issue today in different places that span a continent, and places separated by half a world. In Indonesia, free speech is treated as a crime; political parties are shut down; and labor leaders are thrown in jail. In East Timor brutal repression terrorizes an entire people. In Burma, Nobel Peace Prize winner Aung San Suu Kyi still lives under house arrest while the Burmese people suffer wholesale repression – living in a nation that has become one vast prison. In Southern Mexico, in Chiapas, killing and beating are still tools for silencing those who attempt to bring change. From Cuba to Iran and in nations around the world, oppression is a way of life for millions – and a way of death each year for hundreds of our fellow human beings.

AMERICA'S INTERESTS

The repression of political rights is inevitably combined with the denial of economic rights. And the ripple effects of that denial soon reach deep into the American market. Almost every other country in the world now has virtually unfettered access to our market. Our goal is a world of middle-class consumers eager to buy our products – not a world where low-priced imports flood our market, depressing wages in industries and sectors that have to compete with those imports. We can't compete against workers who have no rights to demand a higher wage in return for their hard work and increased productivity. We can't compete with slave labor.

It's clear that passive efforts to promote greater human rights won't work. Voluntary codes of conduct and other efforts, while often well-intentioned, have had little or no impact. For years the business community has argued that its participation in the economy – simply being there – would yield results. So far, no real progress has been made. We now hear the same arguments for constructive engagement with China that we heard about South Africa. But nothing fundamental changed in South Africa until sanctions came.

If we are to have any credibility among those who believe in America's promise, we must put our money where our mouth is. This Administration has finally placed sanctions on Burma as punishment for its odious human rights record, yet it refused to make the same strong statement when it comes to similar circumstances in Beijing.

The people of the world yearn for a consistent American human rights policy. It is potentially our greatest strength. Those who suffer need to know they are not alone; those who repress need to know that America will not reward their misdeeds. The leverage of our market can and must be a hinge of human freedom. We must remember that the denial of Most Favored Nation trading privileges – and the leverage provided by the Jackson-Vanik Amendment – was part of the "long twilight struggle" that transformed Eastern Europe and the former Soviet Union.

"BUSINESS AS USUAL"

The United States has no business playing "business as usual" with a Chinese tyranny that persecutes Christian and Muslim lead-

ers and leaders from many other faiths, precludes tens of millions from practicing their religion, sells the most lethal weapons to the most dangerous of nations, profits off slave labor, and engages in the utter evil of forced abortion.

I met with the Dalai Lama, now nearing his fortieth year of forced exile from Tibet. Forty years later, dissidents continue to die in detention across that captive nation. Torture, arbitrary arrest, and the closing of monasteries are all common occurrences. The Chinese have attempted to install their own puppet in the Tibetan's second highest religious office. They kidnapped the six year old boy selected by ancient ritual as the next Panchen Lama. That boy is now seven – if he is still alive.

I met with Harry Wu – a real champion of human rights in China. He told me that China's prison camps have become vast profit centers. There's now actually a new term – prison economy. Harry asked: "If America knew that a gulag or concentration camp existed today, you would speak out. Why is America silent now?"

HUMAN ECONOMIC COSTS

It is wrong, deeply wrong, to excuse or rationalize the uncertain gains that come from tolerating the systematic denials of political

OCCUPATION OF TIBET

Since the Chinese invasion in 1949, Beijing has enacted a policy of "population transfer," moving millions of Han Chinese into Tibet, until today Tibetans are a minority in their own country. There are 70 times more Tibetan political prisoners than Chinese, and 30 percent of them are women.

Approximately 20 million people are held in slave labor camps in China and Tibet, earning China hundreds of millions of dollars each year. Infant mortality is 88 percent among Tibetans, as opposed to 31 percent among Chinese. China has devastated Tibet's natural resources by exporting almost all its precious minerals, half of its forests (providing China with $50 billion worth of timber), and using Tibet as a dumping site for Chinese nuclear and chemical waste. After nearly 40 years of primarily nonviolent resistance, the Tibetan people are on the verge of extinction.

Rose Marie Berger, "One Monk, One Yak," **Sojourners**, July/August 1997, 13-14.

and economic rights. What have we gained by trafficking with a tyranny that debases the dignity of one-fifth of the human race? What is gained by a policy that sees all the evils and looks the other way? What is gained by constructive engagement with slave labor? Our trade policy with China has failed. It has failed not only on moral grounds, but economically as well.

There is nothing "free" about our trade with China – in fact it comes to us at great cost and little benefit. Last year, we had an almost $40 billion trade deficit with China. This year it's projected to exceed $50 billion. Between 1989 and 1994, our trade deficit with China increased tenfold, partly because of their strategy of pricing their exports artificially low. They send more than a third of their exports to our shores while less than 2% of our products go there. Today a small nation like Belgium is buying more U.S. goods than China.

A new policy of firm engagement can and must begin when the U.S. Congress reviews Most Favored Nation trading status for China. This market access is a privilege, not a right. I believe that the communist government in Beijing has forfeited that privilege.

It is time we revoke China's Most Favored Nation status.

China and every other country must know that unlimited access to the U.S. market comes with certain responsibilities. Last year was the first year I supported the outright revocation of China's MFN status as our primary policy tool, because it became clear to me that our policies were achieving the opposite of their claimed effect. The State Department's own Human Rights Report paints a bleak picture. We must use MFN as a tool to effect change. MFN is a privilege that has to be earned. Steady, consistent progress by China will enable them to regain this privilege.

READING

21

THE NORTH AMERICAN FREE TRADE AGREEMENT: A SUCCESS

The Clinton Administration

The following appears in the Executive Summary to the Administrative Report of the Study on the Operation and Effects of the North American Free Trade Agreement (NAFTA). As part of the provisions of the agreement between Canada, the United States, and Mexico implemented January 1, 1994, the Clinton Administration released a report to Congress on the impact of NAFTA over the first three years.

■ POINTS TO CONSIDER

1. Define NAFTA and explain why the report was published.

2. According to the report, what impact has NAFTA made on the United States economy? Give examples.

3. Name the other nations in the agreement and describe NAFTA's effect upon them.

4. Opponents of NAFTA cited weak labor and environmental provisions. How does the three-year report respond to these concerns?

5. Discuss the difficulties in measuring the effects of the agreement. Overall, what picture does the report paint of the effects of NAFTA on the United States? Explain.

Excerpted from the Executive Summary to the Administrative Report of the Study on the Operation and Effects of the North American Free Trade Agreement, July 1997.

NAFTA contributed to America's economic expansion.

The North American Free Trade Agreement (NAFTA) entered into force on January 1, 1994. In accordance with Section 512 of the NAFTA Implementation Act, this Study provides a comprehensive assessment of the operation and effects of NAFTA, including the economic effects in aggregate and in selected manufacturing sectors and agriculture, and the implementation of NAFTA environmental and labor agreements. This Study reviews the findings from a variety of outside studies and analyzes Mexican and U.S. data, attempting wherever possible to isolate the effects of NAFTA from other factors, as stipulated in the statute.

TRADE IN NORTH AMERICA

U.S. trade with Canada and Mexico is much larger relative to the size of these economies than with any other trading partners, in large part reflecting shared land borders and geographical proximity.

In 1996, nearly one-third of U.S. two-way trade in goods with the world was with Canada and Mexico ($421 billion). Two-way trade with our NAFTA partners has grown 44 percent since NAFTA was signed, compared with 33 percent for the rest of the world. Mexico and Canada accounted for 53 percent of the growth in total U.S. exports in the first four months of 1997. Canada was in 1993 – and remains today – our largest trading partner, accounting for $290 billion in two-way trade in 1996. Between 1993 and 1996, U.S. goods exported to Canada were up by 33.6 percent to $134.2 billion.

U.S. exports to Mexico grew by 36.5 percent (or $15.2 billion) from 1993 to a record high in 1996, despite a 3.3 percent contraction in Mexican domestic demand over the same period. Exports to Canada and Mexico supported an estimated 2.3 million jobs in 1996; this represents an increase of 311,000 jobs since 1993, 189,000 supported by exports to Canada and 122,000 by exports to Mexico. Exports to Mexico were up by 54.5 percent in the first four months of 1997 relative to the same period in 1993. In the first four months of 1997, U.S. exports to Mexico virtually equalled U.S. exports to Japan, our second largest market – even though Mexico's economy is one-twelfth the size of Japan's.

TRADE BARRIERS

Under NAFTA, Mexico has reduced its trade barriers on U.S. exports significantly and dismantled a variety of protectionist rules and regulations, while the United States – which started with much lower tariffs – has made only slight reductions.

Before NAFTA was signed, Mexican-applied tariffs on U.S. goods averaged 10 percent. U.S. tariffs on Mexican imports averaged 2.07 percent, and over half of Mexican imports entered the United States duty-free.

Since NAFTA was signed, Mexico has reduced its average applied tariffs on U.S. imports by 7.1 percentage points, compared with a reduction of 1.4 percentage points in the United States. The United States would have made some of these tariff reductions under the Uruguay Round even in the absence of NAFTA.

U.S. ECONOMY

Several studies conclude that NAFTA contributed to America's economic expansion. NAFTA had a modest positive effect on U.S. net exports, income, investment and jobs supported by exports. It is challenging to isolate NAFTA's effects on the U.S. economy, since NAFTA has been in effect for only three years, and events such as the severe recession in Mexico, the depreciation of the Mexican peso, and U.S. tariff reductions under the Uruguay Round [of General Agreement on Trade and Tariffs (GATT)] have taken place during the same period.

Nonetheless, several outside studies conclude that NAFTA has resulted in a modest increase in U.S. net exports, controlling for other factors. A new study estimates that NAFTA boosted real exports to Mexico by $12 billion in 1996, compared to a smaller real increase in imports of $5 billion, controlling for Mexico's financial crisis. An earlier study by the Dallas Federal Reserve finds that NAFTA raised exports by roughly $7 billion and imports by roughly $4 billion. The relatively greater effect on exports partly reflects the fact that under NAFTA Mexico reduced its tariffs roughly five times more than the United States. DRI estimates that NAFTA contributed $13 billion to U.S. real income and $5 billion to business investment in 1996, controlling for Mexico's financial crisis.

These estimates suggest that NAFTA has boosted jobs associated with exports to Mexico between roughly 90,00 and 160,000. The Department of Commerce estimates that the jobs supported by exports generally pay 13 to 16 percent more than the national average for nonsupervisory production positions.

THE MEXICAN ECONOMY

In 1995, Mexico experienced its most severe economic recession since the 1930s. Comparing Mexico's recovery in 1996 with Mexico's recovery from its last financial crisis in 1982, when NAFTA was not in effect, reveals that both the Mexican economy and American exports recovered more rapidly following the 1995 crisis than the 1982 crisis, in part because of the economic reforms locked in by NAFTA. Mexico's strong economic adjustment program and bilateral and multilateral financial support were also important.

Following Mexico's 1982 financial crisis, Mexican output drifted down for nearly two years before rising again and did not recover to pre-crisis levels for five years. Although Mexican economic output dropped more quickly in 1995, it also rebounded more quickly, reaching pre-crisis peaks by the end of 1996. Similarly, following the 1982 crisis, it took Mexico seven years to return to international capital markets, while in 1995, it took seven months.

Following Mexico's 1982 financial crisis, Mexico raised tariffs by 100 percent, and American exports to Mexico fell by half and did not recover for seven years. In 1995, Mexico continued to implement its NAFTA obligations even as it raised tariffs on imports from other countries. As a result, American exports recovered in 18 months and were up nearly 37 percent by the end of 1996 relative to pre-NAFTA levels, even though Mexican consumption was down 3.3 percent.

LABOR PROTECTION

The North American Agreement on Labor Cooperation (NAALC) established by NAFTA has, for the first time, created North American cooperation on fundamental labor issues and has enhanced oversight and enforcement of labor laws.

The NAALC submission process subjects member governments to public and international attention for alleged violations of labor laws. The submission process has resulted in such outcomes as recognition of a union previously denied recognition and permitting secret union ballots at two companies where union votes previously were not secret. Between 1993 and 1996, Mexico's Secretariat of Labor and Social Welfare increased funding for enforcement of labor laws by almost 250 percent. Mexico represents a 30 percent reduction in the number of workplace injuries and illnesses since NAFTA was signed.

Under NAALC, the Canadian, Mexican, and U.S. governments have initiated cooperative efforts on a variety of labor issues, including occupational safety and health, employment and training, industrial relations, worker rights and child labor and gender issues.

ENVIRONMENTAL PROTECTION

NAFTA includes mechanisms to address environmental problems that have long challenged communities along the 2000-mile shared border with Mexico. NAFTA's environmental agreements are also encouraging regional cooperation on broader environmental issues and improved enforcement of Mexican environmental laws.

Environmental institutions established under NAFTA are certifying and financing infrastructure projects designed to improve the environment along the U.S.-Mexico border. To date, 16 projects have been certified with a combined cost of nearly $230 million. Construction has already begun on seven projects, including a water treatment facility in Brawley, California, and a water supply project in Mercedes, Texas.

The NAFTA Commission for Environmental Cooperation (CEC) has strengthened trilateral cooperation on a broad range of environmental issues, including illegal trade in hazardous wastes, endangered wildlife, and the elimination of certain toxic chemicals and pesticides. Through the CEC, Mexico has agreed to join the United States and Canada in banning the pesticides DDT and chlordane, ensuring that these long-lived, toxic substances no longer cross our border.

Mexico has established a voluntary environmental auditing program, which has completed audits of 617 facilities to date. Of these, 404 have signed environmental compliance Action Plans representing more than $800 million in environmental investments in Mexico. Mexico reports a 72 percent reduction in serious environmental violations in the maquiladora industry since NAFTA was signed, and a 43 percent increase in the number of maquiladora facilities in complete compliance.

READING

22

THE NORTH AMERICAN FREE TRADE AGREEMENT: A FAILED EXPERIMENT

Economic Policy Institute, et al.

The following article is from a joint report authorized by the Economic Policy Institute, the Institute for Policy Studies, the International Labor Rights Fund, Public Citizen's Global Trade Watch, the Sierra Club, and the U.S. Business and Industrial Council Education Foundation. The report entitled The Failed Experiment: NAFTA at Three Years *was published coinciding with the Clinton Administration Three-Year Report on NAFTA, submitted to Congress, July 1, 1997.*

■ POINTS TO CONSIDER

1. Discuss the issue of trade balance between the United States and its North American trade partners. Contrast this discussion with that of the previous reading.

2. Analyze the article to understand the connection between trade, jobs, and wages, according to the authors.

3. Explain the justification for the devaluation of the peso in Mexico. What do you believe to be the effects of this?

4. Study the labor, environment, and public health concerns raised. Do you believe these concerns have merit?

5. Summarize the conclusions of this piece. Compare and contrast these conclusions with those of the previous reading. What policy directions do these authors suggest?

Excerpted from **The Failed Experiment: NAFTA at Three Years,** by the Economic Policy Institute, the Institute for Policy Studies, the International Labor Rights Fund, Public Citizen's Global Trade Watch, the Sierra Club, and the U.S. Business and Industrial Council Education Foundation, June 26, 1997.

Economic policy is successful only if it produces better lives up and down the income ladder. By this test, the NAFTA approach has failed dismally.

During the debate over the North American Free Trade Agreement (NAFTA), supporters and opponents based their cases largely on divergent predictions of the treaty's likely impact. Supporters expected NAFTA to produce major benefits for the economies of the three signatory countries (the United States, Canada, and Mexico), the living standards of their populations, labor relations throughout North America, and the continent's environment: opponents foresaw worsening problems on all fronts.

Today, the agreement has been in effect for several years. Just as important, the policies of breakneck deregulation that Mexican governments have followed in preparation for greater, NAFTA-style North American economic integration have been in effect for over a decade. Thus, NAFTA has begun to establish a track record. There is no more need to rely on predictions.

The President was required to submit "a comprehensive study on the operation and effects" of NAFTA to Congress. This report reiterates the position taken consistently by the Administration—that the treaty has either fulfilled expectations or is moving steadily in that direction. Indeed, the Administration considers NAFTA to be so successful as to justify its extension to include the entire Western Hemisphere. NAFTA critics strongly disagree.

In this report, several organizations concerned with the well-being of average men and women throughout the continent perform their own evaluation of NAFTA's track record and the economic strategies that produced it...

U.S. WAGES, JOBS, AND TRADE

For nearly two decades, the real wages of American blue-collar workers have been declining. Imports from low-wage countries are an especially important cause of increasing wage inequality, and Mexico is one of America's most important low-wage trading partners.

Between 1993 and 1995, Mexican goods made up 26.7% of the increase of U.S. imports from non-industrialized, low-wage countries. Mexico was also responsible for 43.5% of the increase in U.S. deficits with these countries.Many firms have used the threat of moving to Mexico as a weapon against wage increases and union organization. In a survey commissioned by NAFTA Labor Secretariat, Professor Kate Bronfenbrenner of Cornell found that over half of the firms used threats to shut down operations to fight union organizing drives. When forced to bargain with a union, 15% of firms actually closed part or all of a plant – triple the rate found in the late 1980s, before NAFTA.

In 1996, exports were 36.3% higher to Mexico and 33.4% higher to Canada than in 1993. Growth in U.S. imports from Mexico and Canada, however, was much larger – 82.7% and 41.1%, respectively, over the same period. As a result, a U.S. surplus with Mexico of $1.7 billion in 1993 became a deficit of $16.2 billion in 1996. America's overall deficit with the NAFTA countries hit $39 billion in 1996, an increase of 332% from 1993.

Based on standard employment multipliers, the increase in the U.S. trade deficit with Mexico and Canada has cost the U.S. 420,208 jobs since 1993 (250,710 associated with changes in the trade balance with Mexico, and 169,498 with Canada). NAFTA was responsible for 38% of the decline in manufacturing employment since 1989. NAFTA and globalization generally have changed the composition of employment in America, stimulating the growth of lower paying services industries and accelerating the de-industrialization of our economy.

NAFTA, MEXICO AND THE PESO CRISIS

The 1995 peso crisis is commonly used to excuse the sharp deterioration of the U.S. trade balance with Mexico. However, NAFTA was the foundation for an aggressive export-led growth strategy in Mexico. This assumed that expanding Mexico's exports would create jobs for Mexico's rapidly expanding workforce and steadily increasing living standards. The peso had to fall in order for this strategy to succeed. As Professor Robert Blecker of American University put it, "Mexico had to devalue the peso in order to attract the direct foreign investment and export-oriented manufacturing that NAFTA was designed to promote."

The peso crisis is also intricately linked with the politics of NAFTA. The artificially high peso held down inflation in Mexico, helped to win votes in the U.S. Congress for passage of NAFTA in 1993, and improved the electoral prospects of Mexican presidential candidate Ernesto Zedillo in 1994.

The real value of the peso has been climbing steadily since late 1995 at 5 - 7% per quarter. The Mexican government has been stimulating the economy in advance of coming elections. Past experience suggests that Mexico's next sudden devaluation, and even deeper depression, are only a matter of time.

The peso collapse has devastated Mexico's economy. The number of unemployed workers doubled between mid-1993 and mid-1995, to nearly 1.7 million. Additionally, there were 2.7 million workers employed in precarious conditions in 1996. To make ends meet, many families are forced to send their children – as many as 10 million – to work, violating Mexico's own child labor law. An estimated 28,000 small businesses in Mexico have been destroyed by competition with huge foreign multinationals and their Mexican partners. Real hourly wages in 1996 were 27% lower than in 1994 and 37% below 1980 levels. Of the 1995 working population of 33.6 million, 19% worked for less than the minimum wage, 66% lacked any benefits, and 30% worked fewer than 35 hours per week. During three years of NAFTA, the portion of Mexican citizens who are "extremely poor" has risen from 32 to 51%, and 8 million people have fallen from the middle class into poverty.

CANADA

Canada has been mired in recession since shortly after entering into the U.S.-Canada Free Trade Agreement in 1989. Unemployment increased from 7.5% in 1989 to 11.3% in 1992. Joblessness fell back to 9.4%, but has risen slightly in 1997, to 9.6%. Canada's policies and practices are being harmonized with those of the rest of North America – downward. Between 1989 and 1995, Canada's real interest rate was 2.9% higher than in the U.S. As a result, Canada is cutting government outlays sharply and dismantling its social safety net, while increasing its unemployment rate.

NAFTA AND LABOR RIGHTS

Significant areas of labor rights are excluded from effective review by NAFTA enforcement agencies. To date the North American Agreement on Labor Cooperation (NAALC) has com-

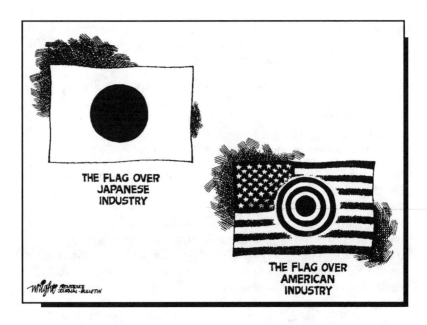

THE FLAG OVER
JAPANESE
INDUSTRY

THE FLAG OVER
AMERICAN
INDUSTRY

pleted only five public reviews of complaints of labor violations. Four of these five complaints have centered upon labor rights violations in Mexico. None of the workers involved in these complaints – more than 200 in total – was reinstated or compensated for serious labor rights violations. A new section is needed in the NAFTA agreement to provide real remedies for labor violations.

THE ENVIRONMENT AND PUBLIC SAFETY

Three years of evidence demonstrate conclusively that the unregulated expansion of North American trade has made an already heavily polluted border region much dirtier and more dangerous; and that the institutions created by NAFTA to handle environmental and public safety problems are utterly inadequate. The NAFTA clean-up plan for the U.S.-Mexico border has failed, generating only one percent of the promised clean-up money. Ozone levels in El Paso have increased steadily since NAFTA. The rate of Hepatitis-A in the border region rose to between two and five times the U.S. average.

NAFTA opened the U.S. borders to trucks that don't meet U.S. safety standards. Fewer than one percent of the 3.3 million trucks entering the U.S. each year are inspected. 50% of those inspected are rejected for major safety violations. NAFTA has weakened food safety inspections. Strawberries, head lettuce, and carrots from Mexico have violation rates of 18.4%, 15.6% and 12.3%, respectively, for illegal pesticide residues.

The Ethyl Corporation of Virginia has filed a $250 million suit against Canadian government, under NAFTA rules, after Canada banned a toxic gasoline additive. If Ethyl wins its case, governments will have to pay polluters not to pollute in order to protect public health.

NAFTA weakened border inspections of U.S. trade. A tragic side effect was to increase the trans-shipment of illegal drugs. Trans-shipment of illegal drugs through Mexico has increased greatly. 80% of the cocaine now entering the U.S. comes through Mexico...

TRUE ECONOMIC GOALS

The organizations behind this report believe that the overriding goal of economic policy should be the creation of conditions that lead to high and rising standards of living, including improvements in environmental quality, health, and social conditions, throughout society. Except as they support this goal, increased employment, reduced inflation, higher productivity, greater volume of trade, even faster overall economic growth cannot be ends in themselves. Economic policy is successful only if it produces better lives up and down the income ladder, and it fails if it does not achieve results. The evidence presented in this report makes abundantly clear that, by this test, the NAFTA approach to North American economic integration has failed dismally. NAFTA should not be extended, but rather repealed or drastically modified.

NAFTA clearly has been good for some North Americans. Exports to Mexico and Canada have produced many new jobs in the United States. U.S. and Canadian investments in Mexico now enjoy strong legal protection. Financial speculators in North America and around the world benefited from a U.S. taxpayer-financed bailout of Mexico. And employers in North America and worldwide have been able to hire workers in the United States, Mexico, and Canada at ever lower wage and benefit levels.

REAL ECONOMIC COSTS

But the costs – to many more North Americans – have been much heavier. Wages and living standards have seen downward

THE REAL SCORE

Clinton did his best to put a happy face on the record, emphasizing that U.S. exports increased by 37 percent from 1993 to 1996, to a record high. But U.S. imports from Mexico have increased more than twice as fast as exports – so fast that we went from a $1.7 billion trade surplus before NAFTA, to a $17.5 billion deficit with Mexico today.

When our imports grow faster than our exports, it drains demand and therefore jobs out of our economy. It's the difference between exports and imports that matters, not just the volume of exports...It is like saying that the Orioles had a very successful game against the Yankees, because they scored seven runs – without mentioning that the Yankees had nine.

Mark Weisbrot, "Clinton's Problem Child: The Ornery NAFTA at Age Three," **Star Tribune**, July 18, 1997.

pressure in all three countries, and workers' rights and bargaining power have been weakened. Damage to the North American environment has intensified. Food supplies are increasingly at risk of contamination. The cross-border trade in illegal drugs has accelerated. For the average citizen of any of the three signatory countries, NAFTA has been a failure.

Rather than produce large and growing U.S. trade surpluses with its neighbors, as proponents guaranteed, NAFTA has plunged America's regional trade into deep and probably chronic deficit. Instead of the promised net new jobs in the United States, NAFTA-encouraged trade and investment patterns have displaced more than 400,000 American jobs on net. Most important, NAFTA has helped to depress U.S. wages and living standards. Workers have been hurt by the availability of cheap labor in Mexico and by great reductions in the bargaining power they hold with their employers. NAFTA's labor side agreement has failed utterly to protect the rights of workers or the enforcement of labor standards. U.S. environmental and public health laws have been subverted, and the quality of the U.S. food supply has been dangerously compromised.

In Mexico, the costs of NAFTA have been even worse. NAFTA-style economics mired the country in slow growth and, after the treaty's passage, led directly to the peso's collapse in 1994. The toll: more than two million lost jobs; 28,000 small businesses destroyed; weaker, less enforceable labor standards and rampant violations of existing worker rights; a rise in already high levels of official corruption; a slowing of the democratic reform process; and the outbreak of revolutionary movements such as that in Chiapas. Indeed, one of the greatest ironies of NAFTA is that a treaty aimed in large part at stabilizing Mexico has heightened social and political disorder. In addition, environmental and public health conditions in the U.S.-Mexico border area have significantly worsened.

Canada's experience, too, has been negative. Canada entered a recession shortly after entering the U.S.-Canada Free Trade Agreement in 1989 and, as a result, has not escaped high levels of unemployment and poor wage growth. Free trade makes impossible Canada's strategy of high social spending and a strong safety net. International financial markets are making Canada pay dearly for this strategy and are forcing its gradual abandonment. Health care, education, and pension systems in Canada are being dismantled in the name of increased competitiveness under NAFTA.

The strategies and rules that produced such results should not be perpetuated, let alone extended. Instead, the entire NAFTA approach to North American economic development should be scrapped. The United States should take the lead in developing new, enforceable rules of trade capable of bringing the benefits of trade expansion to working people throughout North America and eventually the rest of the Western Hemisphere.

READING

23

ENDLESS GROWTH IS OBSOLETE

David C. Korten

David C. Korten has taught at the Harvard Business School and was a former Agency for International Development (AID) advisor and Ford Foundation project specialist in Asia. He is the author of When Corporations Rule the World *(Kumarian).*

■ POINTS TO CONSIDER

1. Define the underlying assumption(s) upon which architects shaped economic policy, in the author's view.

2. Discuss the problems that have grown out of the Bretton Woods vision. How will the continued globalization of the economy impact or address these problems?

3. Explain Korten's belief concerning the market's ability to respond to the various problems discussed in the article.

4. According to the author, describe the effects of globalization on the authority of nations.

5. Analyze Korten's proposed economic alternative to globalization.

David C. Korten, "The Limits of the Earth," **The Nation**, July 15/22, 1996, 14-18. Reprinted with permission from the July 15/22, 1996 issue of **The Nation** Magazine.

Where governments once sought to strengthen market competition through antitrust actions, they now often encourage increased economic concentrations through mergers and acquisitions in the cause of making national corporations "more globally competitive."

President Clinton described the North American Free Trade Agreement (NAFTA) and General Agreement on Trade and Tariffs (GATT) treaties as the cornerstones of his economic and foreign policy and touted them as major accomplishments of his Administration. No more. In his 1996 State of the Union Message he made no mention of either of them.

That tacit acknowledgment of the growing public backlash against economic globalization was echoed only days later at the World Economic Forum's annual meeting in Davos, Switzerland. There, several thousand power brokers of corporate capitalism met under the theme of "Sustaining Globalization." Apparently, the consequences of globalization are proving so devastating that its leading proponents are suddenly deeply worried about public reactions.

MAINTAINING GLOBALIZATION

The concerns of the Davis participants were amplified in a February 1, 1996, *International Herald Tribune* article written by Klaus Schwab and Claude Smadja, respectively founder/president and managing director of the World Economic Forum. With striking candor and insight, Schwab and Smadja noted that "globalization tends to de-link the fate of the corporation from the fate of its employees" and has created a world in which "those who come out on top win big, and the losers lose even bigger." They warned that a "mounting backlash, especially in the industrial democracies, is threatening a very disruptive impact on economic activity and social stability in many countries."

Maintaining that globalization is irreversible, Schwab and Smadja call on political and economic leaders to find ways of demonstrating to the public "how the new global capitalism can function to the benefit of the majority and not only for the corporate managers and investors." Implicit in their supporting recommendations is a belief that this can be achieved through economic expansion fueled by still more public subsidies to business to increase national competitiveness.

While Schwab and Smadja are certainly right about the negative consequences of economic globalization, they are wrong in claiming that it is inevitable or irreversible. Nor can it be made to benefit the majority of people. Its claims and promises are grounded in a flawed ideology that contradicts basic ecological and social realities. A global economy is inherently unjust, unstable and unsustainable.

The removal of barriers to the international flow of goods and money did not happen as part of a natural evolution, as its advocates claim, nor was it the consequence of inexorable historical forces. The policies that made it happen resulted from conscious choices of a self-interested minority who, over the past half-century, have designed, shaped and now control the institutions that dominate global economic activity.

POST-WAR ECONOMIC PARADIGM

The defining movement was the infamous Bretton Woods meeting of 1944, at which the dominant ideologies of globalization – accelerated growth through global free trade and deregulation – were institutionalized. At the opening session, U.S. Secretary of the Treasury Henry Morgenthau advocated rapid "material progress on an earth infinitely blessed with natural riches." He asked participants to embrace the "elementary economic axiom…that prosperity has no fixed limits. It is not a finite substance to be diminished by division."

Thus Morgenthau set forth one of several underlying assumptions of the economic paradigm that has guided globalization since Bretton Woods. Two of these assumptions are deeply flawed. The first is that growth and enhanced world trade will benefit everyone. The second is that growth will not be constrained by the inherent limits of a finite planet.

By the end of this meeting, the World Bank and the International Monetary Fund (IMF) founded, and the groundwork was laid for what later became the General Agreement on Tariffs and Trade (GATT). In the intervening years, these Bretton Woods institutions have held faithfully to their half-century-old mandate. Through "Structural Adjustment Programs," the World Bank and the IMF have pressured countries of the South to open their

borders and convert their economies from diverse production for local self-sufficiency to export production for the global market. Trade agreements like GATT reinforced these actions, opened the global economy to the increasingly free movement of goods and money, and eliminated controls on corporate behavior.

As we look back fifty years later, we can see that economic growth has expanded fivefold, international trade has expanded by roughly twelve times and foreign direct investment has been expanding at two to three times the rate of trade expansion. Yet, tragically, while the Bretton Woods institutions have met their goals, they have failed in their purpose of bringing prosperity to the people of the world. The earth has more poor people today than ever before. There is an accelerating gap between the rich and the poor. Widespread violence is tearing families and communities apart. And the planet's ecosystems are deteriorating at an alarming rate.

LIMITS OF THE EARTH

There is a growing consensus outside official circles that the planet's ecological limits, and the economic injustice inherent in the Bretton Woods system, doom that system to ultimate failure and require a radical change of course.

As the founder of ecological economics, Herman Daly, regularly reminds us, the human economy is embedded in the natural ecosystems of our planet. Until the present moment in human history, however, the scale of our economic activity relative to the scale of the ecosystems has been small enough so that, in both theory and practice, we could afford to ignore this fundamental fact. Now, however, we have crossed a historical threshold. Because of the fivefold expansion since 1950, the environmental demands of our economic system have filled up the available environmental space of the planet. In other words, we live in a "full world."

The first environmental limits that we have confronted and possibly exceeded are not the limits to nonrenewable resources (such as oil), as many once anticipated, but rather the limits to renewable resources and to the environment's "sink functions" – its ability to absorb our wastes. These limits have to do with the loss of soil, fisheries, forests and water; the absorption of CO_2 is being released into the air, and toxins are being dumped into soil and waters. Steeped in market ideology and acutely sensitive to corporate interests, the Bretton Woods institutions have been unable to give more than lip service either to environmental concerns or the needs of the poor. Rather, their efforts have in practice centered on making sure that people with money have full access to whatever resources remain – with little regard for the broader consequences.

RESOURCE DISTRIBUTION

If ecological limits don't doom the Bretton Woods system, growing inequality across the planet will. The United Nations Development Program's "Human Development Report for 1992" introduces the champagne glass as a graphic metaphor for a world of extreme economic injustice. The bowl of the champagne glass represents the abundance enjoyed by the 20 percent of the world population who live in the richest countries and receive 82.7 percent of the world's income. At the bottom of the stem, where the sediment settles, we find the poorest 20 percent, who barely survive on 1.4 percent of the total income. The combined incomes of the top 20 percent are nearly sixty times larger than those of the bottom 20 percent. Furthermore, this gap has doubled since 1960, when the top 20 percent enjoyed only thirty times the income of the bottom 20 percent. And the gap continues to grow.

These figures actually understate the true inequality in the world, because they are based on national averages rather than actual individual incomes. If we take into account the very rich people who live in poor countries and the very poor people who live in rich countries, the incomes of the richest 20 percent of the world's people are approximately 140 times those of the poorest 20 percent. Perhaps an even more startling expression of inequality is that the world now has more than 350 billionaires whose combined net worth equals the annual income of the poorest 45 percent of the world's population. That gap is growing as well.

In his book *The Work of Nations* (1991), Secretary of Labor Robert Reich explained that the economic globalization the Bretton Woods institutions have advanced so successfully has severed the interests of the wealthy classes from a sense of national interest and thereby from a sense of concern for and obligation to their less fortunate neighbors. A thin segment of the super-rich at the very lip of the champagne glass has formed a stateless alliance that defines global interest as synonymous with the personal and corporate financial interests of its members.

This separation has been occurring in nearly every country in the world to such an extent that it is no longer meaningful to speak of a world divided into Northern and Southern nations. The meaningful divide is not geography – it is class.

BOUNDARIES OF THE MARKETPLACE

Behind the ecological degradation and growing inequalities have been several hundred powerful corporations and banks whose scope is now global. By expanding the boundaries of the market beyond the frontiers of the nation-state, corporations have increasingly moved beyond the reach of government. The structural adjustment programs of the World Bank and the IMF and the global free-trade agreements empowered to override national laws have further weakened governments. As a result, real governance has been transferred from national governments, which at least in theory represent the values and interests of citizens, to transnational corporations, which by their nature serve only the short-term interests of their most powerful shareholders. Consequently, societies everywhere on the planet are less able to address environmental and social needs. Meanwhile, ever greater power is being concentrated in the hands of a very few global corporations. Indeed, where governments once sought to strengthen market competition through antitrust actions, they now often encourage increased economic concentrations through mergers and acquisitions in the cause of making national corporations "more globally competitive."

The rapid rate at which large corporations are trimming their work forces has created a misleading impression in some quarters that these companies are losing their power. The Fortune 500 firms shed 4.4 million jobs between 1980 and 1993, but during this same period, their sales increased 1.4 times, assets increased 2.3 times and CEO compensation increased 6.1 times. The average CEO of a large corporation now receives a compensation package of more than $3.7 million per year. Those same corporations employ 1/20th of 1 percent of the world's population, but they control 25 percent of the world's output and 70 percent of world trade. Of the world's hundred largest economies, fifty are now corporations.

The Economist recently reported that five companies now control more than 50 percent of the global market in the following industries: consumer durables, automotives, airlines, aerospace, electronic components, electricity and electronics, and steel. Five corporations control more than 40 percent of the global market in oil, personal computers and – especially alarming in its consequences for public debate on these very issues – media. These companies and others like them are the true beneficiaries of the global economy.

The vision and decisions at the Bretton Woods conference have transformed the governance of societies. Nonetheless, sustainability in a growth-dependent globalized economy is what Herman Daly calls an impossibility theorem. What is the alternative? The answer is the opposite of globalization. It lies in promoting greater economic localization – breaking activities down into smaller, more manageable pieces that link the people who make decisions to the consequences of those decisions. It means rooting capital to a place and distributing its control among as many people as possible.

Powerful interests stand resolutely in the way of achieving such a reversal of current trends. The biggest barrier, however, is the lack of public discussion on the subject. We must begin the process of change by recognizing that our global development models – and their underlying myths – are artifacts of the ideas, values and institutions of the industrial era. Modern corporations have been the cornerstone of that era, concentrating massive economic resources in a small number of centrally controlled institutions. They brought the full power of capital-intensive technologies to bear in exploiting the world's natural and human resources, so that a small minority could consume far more than their rightful share of the world's real wealth. Now, as globalization pushes the exploitation of the earth's social and environmental systems beyond their limits of tolerance, we face the reality that the industrial era is exhausting itself – because it is exhausting the human and natural resources base on which our very lives depend.

READING

24

GLOBALIZATION LEADS TO PROGRESS

Thomas d'Aquino

Thomas d'Aquino is the President and CEO of the Canadian Business Council on National Issues. The following is excerpted from his address before the annual meeting of the Academy of International Business in Banff, Canada, September 27, 1996.

■ POINTS TO CONSIDER

1. Define the author's view of social progress and how globalization is related. Cite evidence from the author to support his view.

2. Discuss the "costs" of globalization and d'Aquino's response.

3. Explain how business acts as an "agent of change," according to the author.

4. Contrast the "old" and "new" images of the multinational corporation.

Thomas d'Aquino, "Globalization, Social Progress, Democratic Development and Human Rights," **Vital Speeches of the Day**, December 1, 1996: 107-110. Reprinted by permission.

At no time in history have the prospects for social progress, democratic development and human rights on a global basis been so favorable.

I would squander an opportunity to engage you in a subject that is not yet at the center of debate in international business but that nevertheless is gaining ground rapidly. I am referring to the impact of globalization on social progress, democratic development and human rights, and to the responsibilities and strategies of companies that find themselves caught up in debate surrounding this issue.

THE MARKET AND SOCIAL CHANGE

Let me begin by asking two important questions. To what extent are the forces propelling globalization consistent with the advancement of social progress, democratic development and human rights? And what should be the responsibilities of companies in reconciling their global trade and investment activities with these goals?

Addressing the first of these questions draws us into a debate about the most extraordinary phenomenon of our times, globalization and the forces propelling it forward, paramount among them trade, investment, capital and technology. In modern history, not since the invention of the steam engine and the onset of the Industrial Revolution in the mid-18th and early 19th centuries, followed by the spread of electric power, mass production and democracy, have we witnessed such a transformation.

The signs of the transformation are all around us: the collapse of the Soviet empire, exploding capitalism in China, Mandela at the helm in South Africa, toppling dictatorships in Latin America, the onset of the digital revolution, the startlingly rapid advance of the Internet, and fiber optics transmitting billions of bits of data per second to every corner of the globe.

With this transformation is rising a new economic, social and political order. The embracing of freer markets by a great part of the developing world is leading to an ever accelerating expansion of global commerce and international investment. Advances in information and transportation services and networks are forging stronger and stronger links between countries, regions, cities, organizations and people. And perhaps most importantly, improving education levels are giving rise to a global middle class that, in the words of Stanford University Professor John Meyer, shares "similar concepts of citizenship, similar ideas about economic progress, and a similar picture of human rights"...

I believe that these forces have been by and large immensely positive. Indeed, I would go further and say that at no time in history have the prospects for social progress, democratic development and human rights on a global basis been so favorable.

Why am I so confident? Because one imperative links trade, investment, capital and technology, the idea of openness, an idea that is on the march and that is virtually unstoppable. In every part of the globe, governments are embracing liberal economic policies. Multinational companies are accelerating the exchange of innovations and people across open borders. Investors are insisting that governments and companies open their books wherever they are and that they practice transparency in their operations. And people, as electors, as consumers, as shareholders, are demanding a higher degree of accountability from both governmental and corporate organizations, and they are getting it.

PRACTICAL EVIDENCE OF PROGRESS

What are some concrete examples of openness in practice? Consider economic growth. The developing world, long mired in stagnation and poverty, has seen enormous progress. From 1988 to 1995, real economic growth in developing countries averaged 5.5 percent, more than double the rate in the industrialized world.

Consider standards of living. The most rapid advancements in standards of living in recent years have taken place in developing and newly industrialized countries. For instance, 12 out of 15 countries ranked by real per capita Gross Domestic Product (GDP) growth between 1990 and 1995 were developing or newly industrialized countries...

Consider exports and imports. The International Monetary Fund points out that between 1988 and 1995, export growth for the developing countries approached an average of close to 9 percent a year, and imports exceeded that number, a far cry from the previous decade when export growth averaged barely 2.5 percent and import growth 4.1 percent.

Direct investment that flows inward are another example. In the

ten years leading up to 1994, foreign direct investment has doubled as a share of global GDP, with the share to developing countries accounting for one-third of the increase; a sign of improving confidence levels on the part of foreign companies in the ability of those countries to offer a stable and attractive economic, social and political environment.

The beneficial social impacts of these economic improvements are captured in the 1996 United Nations "Human Development Report." Two examples are particularly noteworthy: over the past three decades, life expectancy in developing countries has increased more than 30 percent, and primary school enrollment has improved dramatically from 48 to 77 percent.

The effects of this new openness that I have described have been particularly telling in the sphere of political governance. In the past 20 years, the pace of democratization has picked up speed as authoritarian regimes tried in vain to hold back the tide of liberalization...

SHORT-TERM COSTS OF PROGRESS

So far, I have presented a very positive and hopefully convincing case for the economic and social benefits that are flowing overall from the greatly expanded reach of trade, investment, capital and technology. But the story is far from universally rosy. *First,* not all countries have been winners. Much of Africa, for example, and parts of the Middle East, Asia, the Caribbean and Latin America are still saddled with serious economic, social and political problems.

Second, in some countries, notably Russia and some of the former republics of the Soviet Union, the transition from authoritarianism to liberal democracy has been extremely painful, even violent at times. Here we have seen "frontier capitalism" at its worst characterized by corruption, thuggery and abuses of human rights.

Third, there are some countries that in economic terms are winners, but have not yet responded adequately with a relaxation of their political authoritarianism. To them, democracy represents a threat, and they are prepared to use force to uphold the existing order. China and Indonesia are perhaps the best known examples.

And *finally,* there are countries such as Mexico that have made major advances along the difficult road to economic liberalization and democratization only to suffer serious setbacks. Although setbacks are to be expected, they are nonetheless difficult to swallow and painful for the average citizen, who in the case of Mexico has suffered a serious, but temporary, drop in standard of living... While some of those voicing concerns are little more than protectionists and reactionaries in disguise, the negative effects of economic liberalization must be taken seriously.

CATALYSTS FOR DEMOCRACY

The answer to this challenge does not lie in trying to roll back or constrain the forces of trade, investment capital and technology. This would be futile. In part, the answer lies with individual governments ensuring that they pursue sensible domestic policies which couple enhanced competitiveness with effective adjustment programs, and that they respect internationally recognized social and environmental standards. The answer lies as well with multilateral institutions such as the World Trade Organization which must seek to mesh trade investment, the environment and the social dimensions of economic development within its mandate. New and effective international rules governing investment will help, and for this reason it is important to build support for the negotiations on the Multilateral Agreement on Investment.

But responsibility cannot rest only with individual governments and multilateral organizations. Business has a critical role to play, and this brings me to the second of my opening questions. What should be the responsibilities of companies in reconciling their global trade and investment activities with the advancement of social progress, democratic development and human rights? In responding to the question, I will argue a case for responsibility which I believe is relevant to all global corporations. But for illustrative purposes, I will use Canadian companies and the Canadian experience as examples.

Let me begin my response with a broad proposition. Canadian companies should be prepared as a matter of principle to do business in virtually any part of the world save, perhaps, in those few countries that are deemed by the international community to be outlaws. The moral justification for doing business with non-democratic regimes is that trade and in particular direct investment are powerful catalysts for economic liberalization, democratization and the improvement of domestic social conditions...

PROLIFERATING WESTERN VALUES

Canadian companies are by and large excellent agents of change wherever they go because they carry with them sound values rooted in their Canadian experience. The sound values to which I refer are respect for the rule of law, an abhorrence of corrupt practices, respect for workers' rights, a distaste for discriminating practices, acceptance of the importance of safety and health standards, sensitivity to the environment, and an unwillingness to exploit children...

Today, codes of conduct, voluntarily adopted by companies to guide their dealings world-wide, are beginning to gain favor. Levi Strauss and Reebok International are examples. Codes of conduct have certain advantages. The first and most obvious is that they provide policy direction from the boardroom to the frontlines of corporate operations in any part of the world. The second advantage is that they transmit in clear terms to foreign affiliates and to clients the standards by which the company is prepared to do business. Codes will vary from company to company depending on its activities and where it operates. But it is not uncommon for them to set basic standards with regard to safety, health, wages, the environment and forced or child labor.

A final point on what companies can do: companies and in particular the organizations that represent them, are well advised to devote time and resources to helping develop consensus at the multilateral level to advance the cause of social progress, democratization and human rights. Whether at the World Trade Organization, or at the United Nations, a powerful case can be made that a universal acceptance of the rule of law, the outlawing of corrupt practices, respect for workers' rights, high safety and health standards, sensitivity to the environment, support for education and the protection and nurturing of children are not only justifiable within the context of morality and justice. The simple truth is that these are good for business and in most cases lead to enhanced productivity, greater loyalty in the work force, broader community acceptance and ultimately to stronger profitability.

MULTINATIONALS' IMAGE

Despite the manifest logic of what I have just said, some critics here in Canada and plenty of them abroad charge that companies, multinationals in particular, are part of a sinister conspiracy to engage in a "race to the bottom," to destroy social programs, to eliminate workers' rights, to decimate incomes, to exploit children, to foul the environment, to prop up dictatorships. Mercifully, this point of view is much less prevalent than it once was, and increasingly cannot be supported by the facts. Several months ago, *The Economist* summed up the prevailing attitude. "Multinationals," it states, "have shaken off their old sinister image. The United Nations which used to try to control them, now regards them as agents of modernization and good practice. The developing world, having once feared them, now competes to attract their factories. But they are now being judged against the high ethical standards which they themselves helped to propagate."

So there we have it: a world in which an evolved form of democratic capitalism is flourishing, carried forward on the wings of trade, investment, capital and technology with globally-minded, societally sensitive enterprises in the vanguard, supported by billions of independently minded consumers. The picture could not be more encouraging for those of us who have fought long and hard for this kind of world.

But wait, it would be premature to write an "end of history" script and declare that democratic capitalism has irrevocably triumphed. Disparities in all parts of the world are rising. In the United States the costs and benefits of economic liberalization continue to be hotly debated; witness the current *Harvard Business Review* feature entitled "Toward an Apartheid Economy?" Protectionism in increasingly effective forms is rampant in both the developed and developing world. And perhaps most serious of all, political instability is on the rise across the globe fanned by ethnic and religious conflict, and the ability of international organizations such as the United Nations to bring order where there is chaos is severely limited.

This disturbing portrayal of the world and the possibility that the situation will worsen should send a powerful and urgent message to business leaders everywhere. And the message is a simple one: we must work overtime through our enterprises, our business organizations, our governments and our multilateral institutions to give broad and sustained credibility to the new economic order that is emerging. The new order must ensure that the fruits of this new age economic revolution are more fairly and widely distributed on a global basis. If we fail to make this happen, then I expect that the economic revolution I speak of will face counter-revolution probably sooner than we think, and with it will come chaos and disorder on a scale that few today can contemplate. In meeting the challenge, enlightened leadership on the part of business people on every continent will be necessary and in my view decisive.

BIBLIOGRAPHY

Books

Barnet, Richard. **The Global War Against the Poor.** Servant Leadership Press, 1995.

Barnet, Richard and John Cavanagh. **Global Dreams: Imperial Corporations and the New World Order,** 1994.

Barlett, Donald and James Steele. **America: What Went Wrong?** Andrews & McMeel, 1992.

Barlett, Donald and James Steele. **America: Who Really Pays the Taxes?** Simon and Schuster, 1994.

Barlett, Donald and James Steele. **America: Who Stole the Dream?** Andrews and McMeel, 1996.

Chomsky, Noam. **World Orders Old and New.** Columbia University Press, 1994.

Folbre, Nancy and The Center for Popular Economics. **The New Field Guide to the U.S. Economy.** The New Press, 1995.

George, Susan. **How the Other Half Dies: The Real Reasons for World Hunger.** Allenheld, Osmun and Co., 1977.

George, Susan. **The Debt Boomerang: How Third World Debt Harms Us All.** Pluto Press, 1992.

Greider, William. **One World, Ready or Not: The Manic Logic of Global Capitalism.** Simon and Schuster, 1997.

Korten, David. **When Corporations Rule the World.** Kumarian Press, 1995.

Kuttner, Robert. **Everything for Sale.** Alfred A. Knopf, Publishers, 1996.

Phillips, Kevin. **The Politics of Rich and Poor.** Harper Collins, 1990.

Rifkin, Jeremy. **The End of Work: The Decline of the Global Labor Force and the Dawn of the Post-Market Era.** Putnam's Sons, 1995.

Thurow, Lester. **The Future of Capitalism.** William Morrow and Co., 1996.

Zepezauer, Mark and Arthur Naiman. **Take the Rich Off Welfare.** Odonian Press, 1996.

Magazines and Newspapers

Alterman, Eric. "Hope, Again?" **Nation,** 11/25/96, 5.

Bachman, S.L. "Young Workers in Mexico's Economy, **U.S. News & World Report,** 09/01/97, 40.

Bacon, David. "Mexico's New Braceros," **Nation,** 01/27/97, 18.

Baker, S. "Will the New 'Maquiladoras' Build a Better..." **Business Week,** 11/14/88, 102.

Becker, Gary S. "Is There Any Way to Stop Child Labor Abuses?" **Business Week,** 05/12/97, 22.

Brazier, Chris. "Child Labor," **New Internationalist,** July 1997, 1.

Christian Science Monitor. "Palestinians May Cut Child Labor," 02/26/97, 10.

Clifford, Mark L. "Keep the Heat on Sweatshops," **Business Week,** 12/23/96, 90.

Fernandez-Vega, Carlos. "The Changing 'Maquiladora,'" **World Press Review,** Feb. 1994, 44.

Geoghegan, Thomas. "Child Labor in the 1990's," **New York Times,** 12/01/96, E9.

Hazlett, Thomas W. "Kathie Lee & Me," **Reason,** Dec. 1996, 74.

Hilowitz, Janet. "Social Labelling to Combat Child Labour: Some Considerations," **International Labour Review,** Summer 1997, 215.

Juffer, J. "Dump at the Border," **Progressive,** Oct. 1988, 24.

Lansky, Mark. "Child Labour: How the Challenge Is Being Met," **International Labour Review,** Summer 1997, 233.

Lapp, Hannah B. "Labor Department vs. Amish Ways," **Wall Street Journal** – Eastern Edition, 04/10/97, A14.

Malcolm, Teresa. "Children Protest," **National Catholic Reporter,** 08/29/97, 9.

Martin, Justin. "Robert Reich's Labor Pains," **Fortune,** 05/12/97, 162.

Martinez, Demetria. "Victory for Maquiladora Workers," **National Catholic Reporter, 07/29/94, 3.**

McCarthy, Abigail. "Kindler, Gentler Sweatshops," **Commonweal,** 06/06/97, 6.

Multinational Monitor. "Battling Brazil's Child Labor Brutality," Jan./Feb. 1997, 20.

Myerson, Allen R. "In Principle, a Case for More 'Sweatshops,'" **New York Times,** 06/22/97, 5.

Nation. "News of the Weak in Review," 01/06/97, 7.

National Catholic Reporter. "Several Groups Act to Redress Plight of Mexico Workers," 09/17/93, 10.

New Internationalist. "Child Labour – The Facts," July 1997, 18.

New Internationalist. "Confronting Child Labour, Then and Now." July 1997, 26.

New York Times. "The Universal Shame of Child Labor," 12/21/96, 24.

New York Times. "U.S. Says Pizza Hut Broke Safety Rules," 04/10/97, B6.

O'Sullivan, Gerry. "Not-so-free Trade," **Humanist,** Nov. 1992, 1.

Press, Eyal. "Holidays of Conscience, **Nation,** 10/27/97, 7.

Prusher, Ilene R. "Children at Work," **Christian Science Monitor,** 02/26/97, 10.

Reading Today. "UNICEF Month Explores Child Labor Issues, Aug./Sept. 1997, 7.

Tagliabue, John. "Europe Fights Child Labor in Rug Making," **New York Times,** 11/19/96, D9.

Tucker, Lee. "The Small Hands of Slavery," **Multinational Monitor,** Jan./Feb. 1997, 17.

Weissman, Robert. "Stolen Youth," **Multinational Monitor,** Jan./Feb. 1997, 10.

Williams, Walter E. "Feds Destroy Jobs Without Offering Better Alternatives," **Human Events,** 12/20/96, 9.

INDEX

Aquino, Corazon, 41

"Bonded" child, 34

Child Labor Deterrence Act (Harkin Bill), 76

Clinton, William, 26, 149, 154

Convention on the Rights of the Child (CRC), 30, 49-50

Fair Labor Standards Act, 70

Gender gap, 35

General Agreement on Tariffs and Trade (GATT), 58-9

Geneva Convention, additional protocols to the, 48

"Guest worker," 56, 58

Immigration and Naturalization Service, 26-7

International Child Labor Elimination Act, 107-8, 110

International Labor Organization (ILO), 70-1, 88, 104, 108, 122, 128

International Labor Rights Fund, 74

International Money Fund (IMF) and World Bank, 32, 73-4, 86-7, 158

"Jiuye," 13

"Laogaidui," 10-12, 14

"Maquiladora," 95

National Agricultural Worker Survey (NAWS), 65

National Institute for Occupational Safety and Health (OSHA), 75

New world order, 92, 93, 165

North American Agreement on Labor Cooperation (NAALC), 145-6

North American Free Trade Agreement (NAFTA), 27, 88, 130, 157

Operation South PAW (Protecting American Workers), 60

Reich, Robert, 103, 161

Social Clause, 122-3, 126-7, 129, 130

Structural adjustment programs, 73, 86, 158

U.N. Commission of Human Rights, 17

U.N. Declaration of the Rights of the Child, 48

U.N. Human Development Report, 167

UNICEF, 30

U.S. Agency for International Development (USAID), 100

U.S. Census of Agriculture, 63, 64

Wilson, Pete, 56-7

Wilson, Woodrow, 70

World Trade Organization (WTO), 123, 126, 129, 134, 168, 170